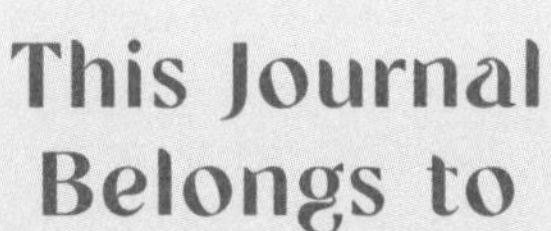

This Journal Belongs to

....

Dena Dyer

The 5-Minute

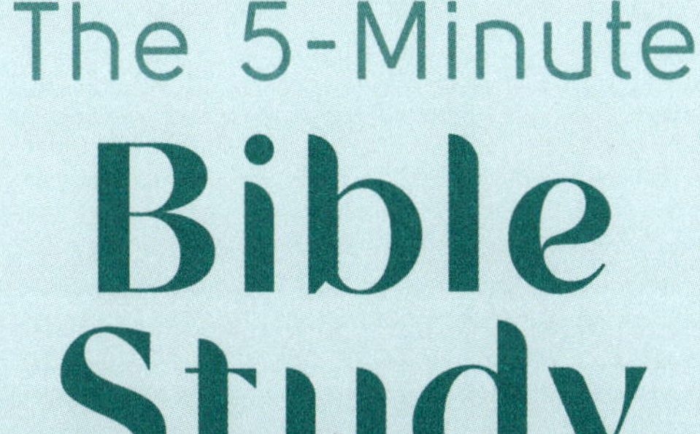

for Moms

YOU are the reason we do what we do here at Barbour Publishing. We promise that we will always use our God-given talents to produce content with you in mind—and that we will remain biblically faithful, no matter what.

Thank you for being the heart of our business.

Print ISBN 979-8-89151-281-8

Text previously published as *The 5-Minute Bible Study for Moms*, published by Barbour Publishing, Inc.

Published by Barbour Publishing, Inc., 1810 Barbour Drive, Uhrichsville, Ohio 44683, www.barbourbooks.com

Our mission is to inspire the world with the life-changing message of the Bible.

Printed in China.

INTRODUCTION:

If you're like many moms, you find it hard to make time for Bible study. You have the best intentions, but busy days turn into packed hours, and before you know it, another week has passed. You know God has treasures stored in His Word for you, but you're also realistic about the demands on your time and energy.

To help make your intentions reality, this book provides a simple and practical way for you to open the Bible regularly, dig into a passage, and journal your thoughts—even if you have only five minutes!

Here's how to use each entry:

- Minutes 1–2: ***Read*** the scripture passage for each day's Bible study slowly and carefully, asking the Holy Spirit to guide and teach you.
- Minute 3: ***Understand.*** Ponder a couple of prompts designed to help you apply the verses from the Bible to your own life. Then journal your answers in the space below so you'll be able to look back on them at another time. Prayerfully consider these prompts throughout your day as well.
- Minute 4: ***Apply.*** Read a brief devotional based on the day's scripture. As you read, think about what you are learning and how to apply the scriptural truths to your own life. Jot down any thoughts or questions that come to mind so you can go back to them when you have more time.
- Minute 5: ***Pray.*** A prayer starter will help you to begin a time of conversation with God. Remember to allow time for Him to speak into your life as well.

The 5-Minute Bible Study Journal for Moms is created to help you to establish the discipline of studying God's Word. Pour yourself a cup of coffee and dive into the riches the scriptures hold.

You will find that even five minutes focused on scripture and prayer has the power to make a huge difference. Soon you will want to make even more time to be in God's Word!

SWEETER THAN HONEY

Read Psalm 119:89–176

KEY VERSE:

How sweet are your words to my taste,
sweeter than honey to my mouth!
PSALM 119:103 ESV

UNDERSTAND:

Think of several words to describe the taste of honey. Have you ever thought to describe scripture like that?

How could you increase your appetite (and your children's appetite) for the things of God?

APPLY:

There's an ancient Jewish tradition in which a child is brought to the synagogue for the first time and given honey as they are instructed in the Torah (the first five books of the Old Testament) by a rabbi. It's believed that a child who tastes honey as they are introduced to the Torah will grasp the concept of God's Word being as sweet as the bees' nectar.

The psalmist wrote chapter 119 out of an immense love for God's Word. To him, it was sweeter than honey. Have you ever thought about making the Bible enjoyable for your children? Do they see you loving the Word or laboring to cross "read scripture" off your daily to-do list?

This week, search out kid-friendly scripture songs, videos, books, and questions. We live in a marvelous time in which abundant, affordable resources are available to us online. Go on a Bible adventure as a family, and perhaps you'll say together: "How sweet are Your words!"

....

....

....

....

....

....

....

....

....

....

PRAY:

Lord, thank You for Your living, active, and powerful Word. As my family and I move through our days, help us savor scripture and feast on Your promises. Remind us to pause for praise during busy seasons. May we say with the psalmist, "Your words are sweeter than honey!"

THE POWER OF WORSHIP

Read 1 Chronicles 16

KEY VERSE:

Ascribe to the Lord the glory due his name; bring an offering and come before him. Worship the Lord in the splendor of his holiness.

1 CHRONICLES 16:29 NIV

UNDERSTAND:

Reflect on attributes of God's character that deserve praise: His mercy, patience, forgiveness, love, etc. Spend some time thanking Him.

How quick are you to worship and praise God during the day?

List a few distractions that draw your attention away from the things of God.

APPLY:

Walking through life as busy moms, we can live distracted from the things of God. Between our kids' schedules, our family's daily needs, and our work inside and outside the home, all our energy gets expended on just living, and we fall into bed wondering where the day went.

However, we don't have to live in a fog. We have a gift from the Creator that can center our hearts and lift our gaze and thoughts to heaven: worship. Nothing gets our mind off our ever-changing circumstances and onto our never-changing God like praising Him for who He is and what He's done.

This week, worship God alone and with your family members by first picking a couple of verses to daily repeat out loud together. Second, begin a family list of answered prayers. Third, keep worship music playing as you do errands or housework—and notice how your spirit lifts.

....

....

....

....

....

....

....

....

....

PRAY:

I confess I often forget to worship You, Lord. Forgive me and create in me a heart that rushes to praise You. Help me be creative and diligent to worship You during the day and as I fall asleep. I know that as I orient my mind and heart around Your goodness and mercy, my spirits will lift and my family will notice the difference.

PEACE IS A PERSON

Read Ephesians 2

KEY VERSES:

But now you have been united with Christ Jesus. Once you were far away from God, but now you have been brought near to him through the blood of Christ. For Christ himself has brought peace to us. He united Jews and Gentiles into one people when, in his own body on the cross, he broke down the wall of hostility that separated us.

EPHESIANS 2:13–14 NLT

UNDERSTAND:

Picture a peaceful scene. Now list several words to describe that scene. How do those words compare to the words you would use to describe your life?

....

....

....

....

Since Jesus brought reconciliation between us and God, as well as (in today's verse) between Jews and Gentiles, we can come near to our heavenly Father in confidence. How might that fact give you peace this week?

....

....

....

....

....

APPLY:

Life is stressful. Whether we're single or married, young or old, or the mom of one or six children, we need peace. However, peace is elusive because our circumstances keep changing and uncertainty is a fact of life. The car breaks down just as we paid it off; the principal calls from the school where our child is being disciplined; our husband gets laid off after we moved cross-country for the job.

But Jesus, in His very last conversation with His disciples before He was crucified, said in John 14:27 (AMP), "Do not let your heart be troubled, nor let it be afraid. [Let My perfect peace calm you in every circumstance and give you courage and strength for every challenge.]"

Notice our Savior didn't tell His followers that peace was available for just a few circumstances but in *every* circumstance. He longs for us to believe this promise and trust in Him fully.

....

....

....

....

....

....

....

....

....

....

....

PRAY:

Jesus, thank You for the promise You gave Your disciples before Your death. I know Your own relationship to the Father gave You courage and strength to face the unthinkable. I now surrender my fears and stress to You, trusting that You are the peace I need for every situation.

SET YOUR MIND ON THINGS ABOVE

Read Colossians 3

KEY VERSE:

Keep thinking about things above, not things on the earth.

COLOSSIANS 3:2 NET

UNDERSTAND:

What "things above" might Paul the apostle be referring to in today's key verse?

....

....

....

....

....

....

In what ways could you remind yourself to lift your gaze to God and His promises and provision more often during the day?

....

....

....

....

....

....

....

APPLY:

The Greek verb in Colossians 3:2 is in imperative form, which is why it's translated in the NET Bible as "keep thinking." Paul was encouraging the church in Colossae to *continually* set their minds on heavenly things.

As moms, do we train our brains to think eternally important thoughts about our relationship to God and Christ, heaven and the gospel, the church, and how we can impact the world for Him? Or do we instead get caught up in momentary middle-schooler meltdowns, teenagers who talk back, and financial frustrations?

One way we can "keep thinking of things above" is to use technology. Set a reminder on your device to pray or praise as the hour changes. When the alarm goes off, pause and say a quick prayer of surrender or thanksgiving. Reorienting our thoughts will pay off in more peace and a kingdom perspective.

....

....

....

....

....

....

....

....

....

....

PRAY:

Father, I long to keep my mind on eternal things instead of earthly ones. Show me how to shift my focus from the daily grind of life to the heavenly future You have waiting for me. As I lift my thoughts to Your kingdom, change my perspective and unite it with Yours.

MADE TO WORSHIP

Read John 4:1–29, 39

KEY VERSES:

"Yet a time is coming and has now come when the true worshipers will worship the Father in the Spirit and in truth, for they are the kind of worshipers the Father seeks. God is spirit, and his worshipers must worship in the Spirit and in truth."

JOHN 4:23–24 NIV

UNDERSTAND:

Jesus debated theology with a woman most people ignored or shunned. That was scandalous for several reasons—among them, because rabbis often didn't talk to women who weren't their wives. She was also a Samaritan, and her people group was despised by the Jews. Why did He engage with her?

....

....

Where we focus most of our thoughts and attention reveals what we treasure most or "worship." If you're honest, what are a few things you might "worship" instead of Jesus?

....

....

....

What's one simple and practical way you could encourage yourself and your children to worship Jesus this week?

....

....

APPLY:

Mom, the truth is: We were made to worship. The question is: *What are we worshipping?* Approval of others? Our children? Netflix? Spouse? Alcohol? Money?

The story of Jesus meeting the woman at the well shows that she was more focused on the *how* and *where* of worship (Jews and Samaritans believed differently about the place they should worship, which caused turmoil between them) rather than the *who* of worship. Truly, when we see Jesus for who He is, we and our children will be transformed, just like the Samaritan woman was. . .and we will then begin to transform the world around us like she did.

Jesus drew the woman at the well—and He wants to draw us—out of isolation and into community, out of shame and into freedom, out of a shallow poverty of spirit and into the riches and depths of His mercy, out of striving and into rejoicing.

....

....

....

....

....

....

....

....

....

PRAY:

Lord, forgive me for so often worshipping other things rather than You. Thank You for making worship more a matter of the heart than of where and how we worship. Help me to see You for who You really are and to show my kids Your character by the way I live. Bring us out of striving and into rejoicing.

EVERY GOOD GIFT

Read James 1

KEY VERSE:

Every good gift and every perfect gift is from above,
and comes down from the Father of lights,
with whom there is no variation or shadow of turning.

JAMES 1:17 NKJV

UNDERSTAND:

List several "good" and "perfect" gifts God has given you. Now list several delightful gifts from nature, such as monarch butterflies, mountain streams, giraffes. . .

....

....

....

....

....

....

What might James have meant when he wrote that God has no "variation or shadow of turning"? What does that mean to you as a mom?

....

....

....

....

....

....

APPLY:

When we're raising kids, it's easy to get distracted. We run from sports practice to school meetings, grocery pickup to our job—and we try to find time for church, our husband, friends, and extended family. No wonder we often keep our focus on to-dos.

What if, for just this week, you instead focused on "ta-das"? Think about those moments God powerfully showed off: with a long-awaited answer to prayer, sweet moment with a child or your husband, or gorgeous sunrise on your commute. By bringing our thoughts around to the goodness of God and His perfect, timely gifts, we reset our minds.

Eventually, gratitude for our generous, faithful Father and His good gifts will become the habit of our hearts. Our family will pick up on this as well, and we may find our home a more joyful and peaceful place.

PRAY:

Holy One, I get so caught up in my list of things to do that I forget to notice the small and large blessings all around me. Thank You for the perfect gifts You give. Change my perspective so I can behold Your light, love, and creativity.

LEAN INTO JESUS

Read Matthew 11

KEY VERSES:

"Come to me, all you who are weary and burdened, and I will give you rest. Take my yoke upon you and learn from me, for I am gentle and humble in heart, and you will find rest for your souls."

MATTHEW 11:28–29 NIV

UNDERSTAND:

What specific things about motherhood make you feel stressed and/or weary?

....

....

....

....

....

....

What life situations feel particularly heavy right now?

....

....

....

....

....

....

....

APPLY:

One of the most comforting aspects of Jesus is that He was fully human as well as fully divine, which means He knew all too well the struggle to keep hope afloat while dealing with weariness, stress, and suffering.

Because Jesus knew weakness, we can approach Him when we keenly feel our own frailty. We can cry out honestly to Him when we feel overwhelmed or running on empty, and He will give us strength to be the patient mom our children need. Even as we pray for job situations to change, financial stress to ease, or loved ones' hearts to soften, we can bow to His will. As we parent, He teaches us endurance and shows us His mercy. Day by day and moment by moment, He builds our faith in His sovereignty.

Leaning into Jesus is the key that unlocks soul-deep rest. As we cling to Him in faith, our children witness our journey toward acceptance and surrender. Who knows how their lives will be changed as a result?

....

....

....

....

....

....

....

....

....

PRAY:

Father, I feel weak and weary so often. Life can be chaotic, and I start to keenly feel my limitations and frailties. Help me to focus on You and cling to Your promises. I lean into You, knowing You will strengthen me and help me endure.

KEEP PRAYING

Read Luke 18:1–8

KEY VERSES:

"And will not God bring about justice for his chosen ones, who cry out to him day and night? Will he keep putting them off? I tell you, he will see that they get justice, and quickly."

LUKE 18:7–8 NIV

UNDERSTAND:

Do you feel as though God views you as a pest when you keep praying about something? What do you think has caused you to believe this?

Jesus told the parable of the persistent widow and contrasted God's character with that of the judge. List some comforting attributes of God's character. How could those characteristics sustain you?

APPLY:

Whether our children are toddlers or teens, they can wear us out with persistent requests and rule breaking. As moms, we may give in out of simple frustration or fatigue.

In today's passage, a persistent widow asked a corrupt, hard-hearted judge over and over to grant her justice, to no avail. However, he eventually gave in to the widow's pleas. Jesus said His Father is the opposite of the judge—just, compassionate, and fair. He encouraged His followers to continue to make petitions, even when answers are not evident or immediate. He related the story to urge His disciples (that's us) to "pray and not give up" (verse 1 NIV).

Take this truth to heart today: God isn't like us, and He doesn't grow tired of our requests. So let's not become weary in praying. If we are praying according to God's will, He hears us and *will* answer in His time and way.

....

....

....

....

....

....

....

....

....

PRAY:

I confess that my humanity colors my perception of You, Lord. Help me to see You as You are. Thank You also for Your Word, which teaches me about Your true character. I will keep praying for those things that remain unanswered. I know You're listening, and I praise You for the way You will answer in Your perfect timing and grace.

SURRENDER YOUR FUTURE

Read Luke 2

KEY VERSE:

[Anna] began praising God. She talked about the child to everyone who had been waiting expectantly for God to rescue Jerusalem.

Luke 2:38 NLT

UNDERSTAND:

When you feel grief or loss, do you turn away from God or toward Him?

Think of one situation in your life that feels heavy and hard. How could you choose worship instead of worry? What difference would surrendering make?

APPLY:

Widowed after only seven years of marriage, Anna devoted herself to worshipping God night and day at the temple and held on to hope that she would see the Messiah before she died. When Joseph and Mary brought the baby Jesus to the temple to be dedicated, she was so close to God that she immediately recognized Jesus as the Promised One, and she spent the rest of her life telling people about Him.

Anna endured eighty-four years of waiting, worshipping, and trusting. Instead of wallowing in grief after her husband died, she held fast to God's promises. Instead of worrying about how she would make it through life as a single woman without resources, she surrendered her entire life to God—and God rewarded her faithfulness.

Friend, no matter how difficult your current circumstances are, God is for you. Resolve to daily surrender any anxiety about the future to the Father who loves you. In doing so, your faith will impact your children—and generations to come.

PRAY:

God, help me to hold on to my faith patiently and joyfully, no matter what life brings. I pray for such a close relationship with You that I immediately recognize You when You are at work around me. May I daily live that faith so winsomely that everyone sees You in me.

YOU ARE CHOSEN

Read 1 Peter 2

KEY VERSES:

But you are a chosen race, a royal priesthood, a holy nation, a people of his own, so that you may proclaim the virtues of the one who called you out of darkness into his marvelous light. You once were not a people, but now you are God's people. You were shown no mercy, but now you have received mercy.

1 PETER 2:9–10 NET

UNDERSTAND:

Do you struggle with jealousy? How does it affect your parenting?

....

....

....

....

....

Does social media affect your mindset as you compare your real life to other women's highlight reels? If so, how could you adjust either your mindset or your social media feeds (or both) to help yourself with this struggle? Pray about your use of social media, and ask the Holy Spirit to reveal whether it is healthy or not.

....

....

....

....

....

APPLY:

Are you ever jealous of other moms? Do their curated social media feeds cause you to wonder if you're doing something wrong? Satan knows that he can use insecurities and doubts about our worth to tempt us to jealousy, envy—even self-hatred. He plants menacing thoughts in our heads: *I'll never measure up. I'm a terrible mom. My children deserve more.*

When we succumb to lies like those, we lose sight of who God has created us to be and what He has specifically called us to do as mothers. However, when we know how much He loves us and remember all that He has given to and planned for us, we can rest secure and cheer others on. We don't have to feel envious or jealous of others' success.

Beloved one, because of who Christ is, we are chosen, holy, called, accepted, and royal. Your children are blessed to call you "Mom," because God chose you just for them.

....

....

....

....

....

....

....

....

....

PRAY:

Lord, forgive me for being jealous of other moms. Thank You for choosing me to be my children's mother. Let me daily renew my mind with Your Word so I can internalize the truth that I am worthy, chosen, called, and accepted because of Your work on the cross.

GOD REDEEMS AND PROVIDES

Read Ruth 1

KEY VERSES:

But Ruth said, "Do not urge me to leave you or to turn back from following you; for where you go, I will go, and where you lodge, I will lodge. Your people will be my people, and your God, my God. Where you die, I will die, and there I will be buried. May the Lord do the same to me [as He has done to you], and more also, if anything but death separates me from you."

Ruth 1:16–17 AMP

UNDERSTAND:

What family relationships are challenging for you? How could you show "noble character" in those relationships?

....

....

....

....

Reflect on Ruth's story. How did God redeem her past and provide for her future? How might He redeem your own journey?

....

....

....

....

....

APPLY:

The book of Ruth was written in Hebrew in the sixth to fourth centuries BC and tells of the Moabite woman Ruth, who accepted Yahweh, the God of the Israelites, as her God. Ruth exhibited such noble character that people took notice. She went from being a destitute widow to the wife of a prominent businessman and the mother of a son who would become an ancestor of Jesus.

One of the most famous passages in scripture is Ruth's declaration to her also widowed mother-in-law that Ruth would never leave Naomi. Through Ruth's story, we learn the importance of prioritizing the relationships God has given us, being bold in faith, and trusting God even when all seems lost.

Mom, keep showing up on behalf of those you love and believing that God will come through for you—even if everything seems to be going wrong. One day you'll be amazed by how God will redeem your story.

PRAY:

Father God, thank You for the plans You have for me and my family. Help me to be a woman of godly character, like Ruth, who is bold and loyal. Give me joy as I serve the loved ones You've given me; and help me develop a deep, abiding faith that You will provide.

PRAYERS AND PERSEVERANCE

Read 1 Samuel 1

KEY VERSES:

"For this boy I prayed, and the Lord has given me the request that I asked of him. So I also dedicate him to the Lord. For all the days of his life he is dedicated to the Lord." Then he bowed down there in worship to the Lord.

1 Samuel 1:27–28 NET

UNDERSTAND:

What things do you pray for during tough times?

What do you think went through Hannah's mind when she left her son at the temple? Why would she put herself through that?

APPLY:

Hannah's suffering did not lead to bitterness but to perseverance. That perseverance formed her character. And her character, forged in the fires of waiting and worshipping, led this woman to dedicate her long-awaited son into God's service.

Do we have this kind of faith, one that isn't fixated on what the world might give but what will most glorify God? Do our prayers focus on us and our problems or on what will give God the honor He deserves? If we're honest, our prayers are probably mostly for financial provision or health for us or our loved ones, instead of for God's glory to be shown and His purposes fulfilled. Our weariness with the dailyness of life tends to crowd out our desire to glorify Jesus.

Let's make Hannah a role model as mothers. Let's refuse to desire lesser things; and instead, let's place our hearts—and our family's lives—securely in the hands of our amazing God.

....

....

....

....

....

....

....

....

....

PRAY:

Forgive me, Lord, for setting my eyes too often on Your lesser gifts—financial peace or health—instead of eternal gifts like godly character, perseverance, and deep faith. Renew my desire to glorify You in every action I take and everything I do for and with my children.

YOUR DIVINE PURPOSE

Read Esther 4

KEY VERSE:

"For if you remain silent at this time, relief and deliverance for the Jews will arise from another place, but you and your father's family will perish. And who knows but that you have come to your royal position for such a time as this?"

ESTHER 4:14 NIV

UNDERSTAND:

Do you ever feel that you lack purpose and are ordinary instead of extraordinary? Why do you think God placed you where you are at this time in history?

Has God asked you to take a bold stand in your job or community? How does that make you feel?

APPLY:

Esther was an ordinary Hebrew woman who became queen of Persia. Because of her resourcefulness and courage, she thwarted a genocide of her people. Esther didn't let fear get in the way of speaking out on behalf of others. And her story is now celebrated as a Jewish festival (Purim) and is included in the Old Testament.

Esther reminds us that we have been placed where we are, in this season, for a reason. God has made us a part of the "royal priesthood" in Christ, with divine purpose and influence within our families and communities. Remember that even when it seems no one is listening to you, your voice matters.

Whether God calls you to stand up for your children, husband, faith, or those in need, the Holy Spirit can give you the boldness to be obedient, no matter the cost. Who knows what amazing things God will bring out of your faithfulness?

....

....

....

....

....

....

....

....

....

PRAY:

Father, I confess sometimes my role seems so small. Forgive me for often being discouraged by the "ordinary-ness" of my life. I thank You for the place of influence I have in my family. May I be bold in Your power to lead them as a compassionate and courageous servant, with Jesus as my example.

WHEN YOU FEEL INVISIBLE

Read Luke 10

KEY VERSES:

But Martha was distracted with all the preparations she had to make, so she came up to him and said, "Lord, don't you care that my sister has left me to do all the work alone? Tell her to help me." But the Lord answered her, "Martha, Martha, you are worried and troubled about many things, but one thing is needed. Mary has chosen the best part; it will not be taken away from her."

LUKE 10:40–42 NET

UNDERSTAND:

Do you ever feel invisible or unappreciated as a mom? What makes you feel that way?

....

....

Name several sacrifices your mother or another relative made for you and what that meant in your life.

....

....

....

How could spending time with Jesus help you gain a different perspective on mothering?

....

....

....

APPLY:

Motherhood can be a thankless task. Our efforts often go unnoticed by the ones we love, and it can start to wear us down emotionally, mentally, and physically.

Let's be encouraged by Martha. She often gets criticized because she was impatient with her sister Mary who sat at Jesus' feet listening to the Lord teach while Martha worked in the kitchen. However, Martha obviously had a sense of justice and fairness, and her gifts of service and hospitality provided a respite for Jesus and His disciples during His earthly ministry.

As a mom, when your children need help, you run into action to serve them. Don't allow the enemy to let you think that your efforts are overlooked, insufficient, or unneeded. Your labor is never in vain. Your gifts and generosity are not an accident.

Continue to serve the Lord wholeheartedly by giving of yourself. Know that your ability to meet needs and sacrifice your comfort serves as a form of worship.

....

....

....

....

....

....

....

....

....

PRAY:

I get discouraged, Lord, by the ways my family seems to take me for granted. Help me to see my role as a mother the way You see it: an opportunity to live out servanthood in front of the people I love the most. May my sacrifice be an offering of praise to You.

FIND A MENTOR

Read Judges 4

KEY VERSE:

She would sit under the palm tree. . . . And the children of Israel came up to her for judgment.

JUDGES 4:5 NKJV

UNDERSTAND:

Whom do you go to for advice about parenting when you aren't sure what to do? Is that the best person or source to turn to?

Which older women do you admire? Why?

APPLY:

From the moment we announce a pregnancy, moms are under intense scrutiny. People want to tell us what's the best feeding, sleeping, or discipline method. For first-time moms, the pressure can be intense and the input confusing. That's why it's important to have at least one older, wiser woman to go to for questions and advice.

Deborah, who is the only female judge listed in the Old Testament, served the Israelites as a prophet, judge, military leader, and songstress. (Impressive list, right?) Scholars say the palm tree she sat under serves as a symbol of peace, fruitfulness, grace, and elegance. Don't you aspire to have a home with those qualities? You can.

Find a woman like Deborah in your church or community and ask her to be a resource or even mentor you. As a woman longing to parent in a godly way, you need other godly women in your corner. They can help you make wise decisions and develop sound judgment.

PRAY:

Father, I long to have a home full of peace and grace, but sometimes I'm overwhelmed with information and advice. Guide me to a godly woman like Deborah who can be my friend and mentor on this road. As I gain experience and wisdom, help me to be that resource and sounding board for someone else.

GOD IS A SAFE PLACE

Read Proverbs 18

KEY VERSE:

The name of the LORD is like a strong tower;
the righteous person runs to it and is set safely on high.
PROVERBS 18:10 NET

UNDERSTAND:

What worries keep you up at night or cause you to fret during the day?

What promises from God could settle your heart when you feel anxious? Write several on index cards and put them in prominent places around your home so you can read them frequently and keep your mind focused on biblical truth.

APPLY:

Most moms know the feeling of utter disbelief when the hospital releases you to go home, placing the small bundle in your arms for safekeeping—for life.

We naturally feel concern about our children's safety from the moment we know they exist. However, the Bible repeatedly tells us not to worry. How can we do that?

Today's scripture provides a clue. The NET Bible commentary on Proverbs 18:10 says, "The metaphor of 'running' to the Lord refers to a wholehearted and unwavering trust in God's protection." When we feel ourselves getting anxious—whether after we read or watch the news or just kiss our child goodbye for any period of time—we can determine to meditate on God's promises and trust He will keep them.

Next time you feel the seeds of worry trying to sprout, read scriptures that talk of God's faithfulness and protection. Then repeat as necessary.

PRAY:

Father, forgive me for so often worrying about things I can't control. Help me to remember that You are with me and my children and that nothing can separate us from Your love. I long to trust You wholeheartedly and unwaveringly. Develop in my heart that kind of faith.

LEAVE A GODLY INHERITANCE

Read Proverbs 13

KEY VERSE:

A good person leaves an inheritance for his grandchildren,
but the wealth of a sinner is stored up for the righteous.
PROVERBS 13:22 NET

UNDERSTAND:

When you think of an inheritance, what images come to mind? Have you ever gotten an inheritance?

....

....

....

....

....

....

What kind of inheritance (financial or otherwise) do you want to leave your children and grandchildren?

....

....

....

....

....

....

APPLY:

Most of us think of money when we hear the word *inheritance*. The NET Bible commentary on Proverbs 13:22 states: "In ancient Israel the idea of leaving an inheritance was a sign of God's blessing; blessings extended to the righteous and not the sinners."

Thankfully, God showed us through the ministry of Jesus that God's blessing extends to the unrighteous as well.

But in another way, today's scripture is true. Think of *inheritance* more like *legacy*. Ask yourself what kind of family culture you're leaving for your kids. Are you passing on patterns learned in dysfunctional relationships? Do you model a servant-hearted faith that loves others sacrificially—or do your children see you putting your needs and convenience first?

As moms, we have a huge influence on our home's tone. Pray for wisdom on making it more spiritually, mentally, and emotionally healthy so you can leave a generous inheritance of wholeness, peace, and joy.

....

....

....

....

....

....

....

....

....

PRAY:

Father, I admit I've mainly thought of inheritance in terms of money. I want to make wise decisions with our family's finances, but also help me to think about the entire legacy—spiritual, emotional, and mental—I'm leaving to my children. May it be one that reflects and glorifies You.

THE SECRET TO CONTENTMENT

Read Philippians 4

KEY VERSE:

I can do all things through him who strengthens me.

PHILIPPIANS 4:13 NRSVA

UNDERSTAND:

In what areas do you struggle with being content: Possessions? Career? Family?

How could you consciously connect with Christ today?

List ten things for which you're grateful.

APPLY:

Have you ever heard Philippians 4:13 quoted at the beginning of a church building program or an athletic event? You may have said it to yourself when trying to achieve a health or work goal.

Yes, God desires to help us do all things in His name and for His glory. However, in context, the verse takes on a new light. Paul notes that he has learned to be content in every circumstance—not through mastering his emotions on his own but through Jesus Christ, who gives him strength.

Just as we can't be good enough for God to save us, we can't muster up contentment on our own. Instead, we must consciously, daily connect with Christ and allow him to work contentment into our lives, like a baker works yeast into dough. As we submit our "wants" to Jesus, He refines them until we desire what He desires and nothing more.

PRAY:

I confess I struggle with being content. I've tried to do it on my own for too long. Forgive me. Today, heavenly Father, I ask You to center me. Give me eyes to see how blessed I am. I want the world to know—by the peace in my heart—that I have everything I need in You.

GOD'S LIMITLESS LOVE

Read Philippians 3

KEY VERSES:

Yes, everything else is worthless when compared with the infinite value of knowing Christ Jesus my Lord. For his sake I have discarded everything else, counting it all as garbage, so that I could gain Christ and become one with him. I no longer count on my own righteousness.

PHILIPPIANS 3:8–9 NLT

UNDERSTAND:

Have you tried to earn God's approval? How?

....

....

....

....

....

....

Is it hard to accept that Jesus' love for you is infinite and not based on your actions? Why or why not?

....

....

....

....

....

....

....

APPLY:

Do you serve God because you don't want Him to be disappointed in you, much like our children often obey because they don't want to reap the consequences of breaking household rules? Or do you serve Him out of the overflow of love you have for Him?

It's easy to give lip service to God's grace, but it's harder to live by it. Do you believe at your core that God's love is limitless and that you can't earn an iota of it? When you do, instead of being bound to a list of rules to follow, you'll begin serving God out of gratitude for all He accomplished on the cross.

When you and I understand how much God loves us and the depths to which He went to rescue us, we'll desire to make Him the priority. We'll count everything else as "loss," like Paul did, to get closer to the lover of our souls. And that relationship will become our greatest joy.

PRAY:

Jesus, thank You for giving of Yourself so that I could be freed from the bonds of sin and death. I can't even put into words how grateful I am. Forgive me for trying to win Your approval by my works. I know now that I can do nothing to make You love me more—or less.

REST IN CHRIST

Read Psalm 62

KEY VERSE:

Truly my soul finds rest in God; my salvation comes from him.

PSALM 62:1 NIV

UNDERSTAND:

What does it mean to rest in God? List a few qualities of someone who rests in Him.

....

....

....

....

What tempts you to give up hope and instead be filled with despair?

....

....

....

....

Have you ever struggled with depression? If so, have you sought help for it?

....

....

....

....

....

APPLY:

When school shootings fill news reports, natural disasters strike, and nations engage in war, we're inundated with uncertainty, fear, and doubt. When we give in to the lie that it's all for naught and there's no reason to hope, depression descends, and our future looks bleak.

Today, stay away from news and social media and notice if it helps you be less hopeless. Determine to surround yourself and your children with worship music, biblical truth, and people who teach that truth regularly. And don't be afraid to ask for help if you need assistance pulling yourself out of an emotional hole. God has given us tools to win the battle against despondency, including godly therapists, medicine—and especially His eternal Word.

Instead of focusing on what-ifs, we can fix our mind on God's character, His promises, and the new life Jesus gives. Over time, as God's Spirit ministers to us and our habits change, we will find joy filling the former dark spaces.

....

....

....

....

....

....

....

....

....

PRAY:

Lord, I want a heart at rest. Show me the best way to find, keep, and sustain peace. Thank You for the tools You give us to fight despair and depression. Build in me the discipline to fill my mind and heart with Your good news—and to teach my children to do the same.

THE POWER OF QUESTIONS

Read John 14

KEY VERSES:

"And if I go and prepare a place for you, I will come back and take you to be with me that you also may be where I am. You know the way to the place where I am going." Thomas said to him, "Lord, we don't know where you are going, so how can we know the way?"

JOHN 14:3–5 NIV

UNDERSTAND:

Do your children ask a lot of questions? How does that make you feel?

....

....

....

....

....

....

Do you think you can ask God questions? Why or why not?

....

....

....

....

....

....

APPLY:

Children ask *so* many questions: "Would you rather have no pinkie toe or no big toe?" Kids also think deeply at times: "Who invented written words? And why did they do that?" We must sometimes dig deep to patiently respond.

It's easy to get frustrated by their unending queries, but what if we instead took their questions as invitations to a closer relationship? When we take even their silly questions seriously, we show that we value their thoughts.

Did you know that God treasures our honest questions? The Son of God didn't smite a disciple when he expressed his doubts; instead, He showed up and invited Thomas to feel His scars. Jesus also asked great questions of His followers and those who were drawn to Him in either curiosity or suspicion. Resolve to thoughtfully (or at least patiently) answer your children when they throw out queries. And go to God in prayer with your own questions, knowing He is leaning in to listen.

....

....

....

....

....

....

....

....

PRAY:

Father, just like my children have questions for me, I have so many questions for You. Thank You for not turning me away when I have doubts or need reassuring. Give me a heart like Yours so I can draw my children close when they ask me questions and invest in the relationship.

HOLY HOUSEKEEPING

Read Colossians 3

KEY VERSES:

Whatever you do, do it enthusiastically,as something done for the Lord and not for men, knowing that you will receive the reward of an inheritance from the Lord. You serve the Lord Christ.

COLOSSIANS 3:23–24 HCSB

UNDERSTAND:

What is your attitude toward repetitive household tasks? Do your kids mirror your actions?

How could you change your mindset toward chores? What might be the result?

APPLY:

Do you rush through tasks like cleaning, laundry, and dishes? Many of us see chores as something to get through on our way to have fun with our kids or put up our feet.

There's another way to live, however. We can view housekeeping tasks with gratitude instead of grumbling and use them as moments of reflection. Next time the dishes need scrubbing, turn on some instrumental music and pray for the people who used each fork, plate, or bowl. Do the same as you fold and put away clothes and towels. There can be something soothing and meditative, even holy, about serving our families.

When we view daily habits as opportunities for transformation, God works through and in us in startling ways. His redeeming work quietly and consistently hones our motives, changes our attitudes, and orders our days according to kingdom priorities. Our routines then become windows of grace through which we see Him more clearly.

PRAY:

Father, forgive me when I have a negative attitude toward housekeeping. Instead of being thankful for the home You've provided, I gripe about the upkeep it entails. Show me a different way to go about my routines, and help me teach my children the joys of simple, worshipful service.

OUTSIDER NO MORE

Read Psalm 80

KEY VERSES:

Stir up your might, and come to save us! Restore us, O God; let your face shine, that we may be saved. O Lord God of hosts, how long will you be angry with your people's prayers? You have fed them with the bread of tears, and given them tears to drink in full measure.

Psalm 80:2–5 NRSV

UNDERSTAND:

When was the last time you felt like an outsider? How does the truth of Jesus pursuing those outside the mainstream—even becoming one of them—comfort you?

Do you have someone in your life who's an outsider to whom you could send a note of encouragement?

APPLY:

Most likely, all of us have felt like an outsider at one time or another. When other moms form a clique and exclude us, it stings. When friends have a gathering without us and post about it on social media, it makes us feel rejected. And when our children get left out of parties, proms, or playground games, it hurts us as much as it hurts them.

Jesus was born outside an inn and worshipped by shepherds who were outside the mainstream of society. He called smelly, poor fishermen, a violent political activist, and a despised tax collector to be his closest followers. He spent time with women, Gentiles, Samaritans, and sinners. He died an outsider, and His last act before He died on the cross was pardoning a condemned man.

We were once outsiders, but no longer. We have unending peace and eternal security—gifts which we should share with others who need them.

....

....

....

....

....

....

....

....

....

PRAY:

Lord, thank You for coming to rescue me from a life of sin so that I could come inside Your kingdom. When my children or I face opposition, ridicule, or rejection, impart Your peace. Let Your face shine on us, and help us to shine Your light to others who feel lonely and isolated.

STRONG-WILLED KIDS (AND MOMS)

Read Proverbs 22

KEY VERSE:

Teach a youth about the way he should go;
even when he is old he will not depart from it.
PROVERBS 22:6 HCSB

UNDERSTAND:

Are you in the middle of raising a strong-willed child? If so, what are the hardest things about it?

....

....

....

Are there any positives about your child's strong will? (For instance, might they resist peer pressure and be their own person when they get older?)

....

....

....

What might God want to teach you about Himself through mothering a child with a strong will?

....

....

....

....

APPLY:

If you have the enormous challenge of raising a strong-willed kid, know there is hope. Pray for God to give you a support network, and don't be afraid of asking for help. Seek out biblical wisdom and helpful resources. Ask God to help you move toward your child in love—even when they reject or mistreat you.

Finally, consider what author/speaker Debbie Williams wrote in *The Plan A Mom in a Plan B World*: "Perhaps you've never thought of Jesus as being a strong-willed child. I beg to differ. . .Jesus' strong will is evident not only in what He did but also in what He didn't do. He's our model of a strong-willed individual standing against fleshly desires and being obedient to His Father's will."

Take heart, momma. This child you are mothering may test you at every turn, but God is big enough to handle your fears and concerns. He will uphold and guide you faithfully.

PRAY:

I thank You, Father, for being patient with me when I don't obey. Help me to have godly patience and endurance as I parent the child(ren) You've given me. I desperately need Your strength and wisdom. I want to emulate Your goodness, peace, and joy as we walk through life together.

HE REJOICES OVER YOU

Read Zephaniah 3

KEY VERSE:

"The Lord your God is in your midst; he is a warrior who can deliver. He takes great delight in you; he renews you by his love; he shouts for joy over you."
ZEPHANIAH 3:17 NET

UNDERSTAND:

What gives you joy as a mom? List a few things, like when your children say "I love you," when you see them succeeding, etc.

Have you ever thought about the joys you bring to your heavenly Father? What might those be?

Do you ever find yourself fighting God about changes and challenges in your life? How might you learn to rest in Him and be renewed by Him?

APPLY:

One of the sweetest times as a mom is rocking our babies when they are small, holding them close to our hearts. We delight in their smell and soft skin, kiss their chubby cheeks, and coo over them with silly songs.

Did you know the Word of God pictures God delighting in us the same way? The key verse today says He does—with shouts of joy.

When Jill's son Jayden was a baby, he fought hard against going to bed. She sometimes had to literally restrain him in her arms to get him to go to sleep. She would sing softly with her arms holding him tightly so that he couldn't squirm away. He cried in frustration but would ultimately succumb to fatigue.

Not only does God delight in us, He also holds us even when we're fighting Him. His Word quiets our spirit as His Spirit renews our heart.

PRAY:

I can scarcely believe that You shout over me with joy, yet that's just what Your Word says. Thank You, Father, for allowing me to be Your child. Thank You also for holding me to Your heart even when I'm trying to fight against You. Quiet my spirit and renew my heart.

HE CARRIES YOU

Read Isaiah 63

KEY VERSE:

In all their distress he too was distressed, and the angel of his presence saved them. In his love and mercy he redeemed them; he lifted them up and carried them all the days of old.

ISAIAH 63:9 NIV

UNDERSTAND:

In what areas do you feel weak or unequipped as a mom? What specifically makes you feel that way?

How does it make you feel to realize God will redeem all your mistakes and carry you through all your years?

APPLY:

No matter what stage of motherhood you find yourself in, there are difficulties. Toddlers challenge us physically with their energy level, constant questions, and lack of consistent sleep schedules, while older children challenge us emotionally. Tweens, teens, and young adults need our assistance transitioning from dependency to independence in every area. We teach them to drive, handle a job and finances in a mature way, and navigate relationships. It's enough to make your head spin.

Thankfully, we don't have to handle parenting on our own. God has given us His Word, Spirit, and church as support for our earthly challenges. He loves our children more than we do and hurts when we hurt. He promises to redeem all wrongs; He gives us wisdom, discernment, and mercy as we imperfectly raise the kids He's given us. And whether we have a supportive husband or not, He holds us in our sorrows, lifts us up, and carries us when we're weak.

....

....

....

....

....

....

....

....

....

PRAY:

Sometimes, Father, I feel so ill-equipped in this parenting journey. Thank You for providing Your people, the Holy Spirit, and scripture to help me, for lifting me up when I'm hurting, and for carrying me when I'm weak. Give me Your strength, wisdom, and discernment in every stage of motherhood.

PEACE THAT PASSES UNDERSTANDING

Read Colossians 3

KEY VERSES:

Let the peace of Christ rule in your hearts, since as members of one body you were called to peace. And be thankful. Let the message of Christ dwell among you richly as you teach and admonish one another with all wisdom through psalms, hymns, and songs from the Spirit, singing to God with gratitude in your hearts.

COLOSSIANS 3:15–16 NIV

UNDERSTAND:

Who is the umpire in your mind, meaning who decides what goes in and what stays out—the world, friends, culture, or social media?

....

....

....

....

....

What are some lies you've been believing? Write them down and then release them to God in prayer.

....

....

....

....

....

APPLY:

In today's passage, the Greek in verse 15 literally means "*let peace be the umpire of your minds.*" Picture an ump in black-and-white stripes behind home plate as thoughts like *God is disappointed in me* swing a bat over home plate. The umpire shakes his head, jerks his right hand over his head, and shouts, "You're OUTTA HERE!"

Friend, when erroneous thoughts try to take up root in your minds, you can compare them to the truth of the Bible and see them for what they are.

As you ponder Colossians 3:15–16, ask God to show you any lies you've allowed to take root. Journal a prayer of confession and gratitude to Him. You might even look up a worship song that speaks to your heart and sing it out loud to Him, praising God who gave His Son (the Word made flesh) to set us free.

....

....

....

....

....

....

....

....

....

....

....

PRAY:

Lord, I'm grateful for Your peace that truly passes understanding. I'm also thankful You keep me supernaturally wrapped in that peace when I focus on You. Help me recognize the lies of the enemy so I can also help my children know and remember the truth.

INSECURE NO MORE

Read Romans 12

KEY VERSE:

Don't copy the behavior and customs of this world, but let God transform you into a new person by changing the way you think. Then you will learn to know God's will for you, which is good and pleasing and perfect.

ROMANS 12:2 NLT

UNDERSTAND:

Do you ever feel insecure? If so, in what areas are you most likely to feel this way?

....

....

....

How might seeing your life from God's perspective help you to feel more secure?

....

....

....

Ask God to transform your mind so you can see how He sees and do what He is asking of you—no more, no less.

....

....

....

....

APPLY:

While scrolling on Instagram, we see "influencer" moms who seem to have it much more together than we do—with immaculate houses, natural diets for their families, and a cache of money to spend on their broods.

It's a constant war not to let the "how good of a mother am I?" questions run away with our emotions—and our peace. Maybe you can relate. Insecurity seems to be an epidemic right now among women of all ages. With social media providing curated highlights of other moms' lives, we can find ourselves defeated before we finish our first cup of coffee in the morning.

However, God wants us to live confidently in His grace, not second-guessing ourselves every moment. With His help, we can quiet the "shoulds" and focus on what He's asking us to do. Because of Him, we can rest assured that we are accepted and secure—just the way He made us.

....

....

....

....

....

....

....

....

....

PRAY:

I praise You, Father, for accepting me just as I am while still changing me into more of who You want me to be. Forgive me for letting the world affect my mind more than Your Word does. Transform my thoughts and give me Your perspective on my life. I surrender to You.

PEACE IN THE CHAOS

Read Isaiah 26

KEY VERSE:

You will keep in perfect peace those whose minds are steadfast, because they trust in you.

ISAIAH 26:3 NIV

UNDERSTAND:

Do you struggle with making time for focusing on God and His Word?

How could you find a few minutes here and there to read the Bible or pray?

APPLY:

The book of Isaiah is a perfect book to turn to when you're feeling fearful, frustrated, or frazzled. Take the key scripture today, for example. We can be comforted by sitting with the Word and stilling our minds in God's presence (even if we must steal five minutes at the very end or beginning of the day). We may not hear an audible voice or bells ringing, but something supernatural happens when we open the scriptures. We regain our composure and reset our mindset as the Holy Spirit quiets our souls.

Time with God amid the chaos of parenting helps us to realize we're doing the best we can in the roles we've been given with God's strength, wisdom, and help. Our best is enough for Him.

We need those daily moments with our Maker to remind us that our children are not burdens to be born—they are our biggest blessings.

PRAY:

Thank You for making me a mom, Lord. I want to see my kid(s) as my biggest blessing, not as a burden. Give me creativity and discipline to reorient myself around Your holy Word daily. I need Your wisdom and strength to be a blessing to this family that You've graciously given me.

REGAINING A SENSE OF WONDER

Read Job 37

KEY VERSES:

"Listen to this, Job; stop and consider God's wonders. Do you know how God controls the clouds and makes his lightning flash? Do you know how the clouds hang poised, those wonders of him who has perfect knowledge?"

Job 37:14–16 NIV

UNDERSTAND:

When was the last time you stopped and gazed in wonder at a glory in nature, a fellow human's accomplishment, or a spiritual truth?

How could you cultivate wonder in your daily life? Might your children lead the way in making wonder more of a spiritual practice?

APPLY:

A mom's life is full to the brim with calendar notifications, the expectations of others, and a myriad of activities. Then there are bills, bills, and more bills. It's enough to make the most easygoing mother a bit grumpy.

Do you know what the best cure for grumpiness is (whether in ourselves or our kids)? Wonder. Our children are experts at this trait. They stop to marvel at a caterpillar crawling on the ground or find beauty in the sun's reflection on a puddle in the driveway. The next time your child slows down in wonder, stop, kneel down, and let your child teach you what we as adults have forgotten: God puts beautiful surprises in our path. We've simply grown out of noticing them.

"This, surely, is the most valuable legacy we can pass on to the next generation," wrote Arthur Gordon in *A Touch of Wonder*. "Not money, houses, or heirlooms, but a capacity for wonder and gratitude, a sense of aliveness and joy."

PRAY:

Holy Father, thank You for the innate sense of wonder my children have. Help me, even on tough days, to slow down and let them—and You—teach me. Give me a new sense of awareness so I can build my capacity for wonder and live with gratitude and overflowing joy.

ABIDING IN CHRIST

Read John 15

KEY VERSE:

"Abide in me, and I in you. As the branch cannot bear fruit by itself, unless it abides in the vine, neither can you, unless you abide in me."

JOHN 15:4 ESV

UNDERSTAND:

When you think of the Holy Spirit, what comes to mind?

What does your church teach about the Holy Spirit? How often is He mentioned?

Are you good at dwelling and enduring when your faith is tested?

APPLY:

Jesus gave His disciples the message in John 15 right before His cruel death. The Greek word for *abide*, which He used many times in the passage, is *meno*—which means to "stay" or "remain." Strong's Concordance also gives these synonyms for the word: *continue*, *dwell*, *endure*, and *stand* (among others).

The disciples didn't endure or stand when He was arrested, tried, and put to death; instead, many of them fled in fear. Yet after His resurrection and ascension, they boldly preached the gospel—and most were martyred for their faith. The difference was this: Jesus gave them the Holy Spirit upon His ascension. They had seen His miracles, but not until they were indwelt with His presence could they obey what He was asking and live fruitful lives.

It's the same with us. Because of the Holy Spirit, we can abide in Him and bear much fruit as mothers. Aren't you thankful you don't have to "mom" alone?

....

....

....

....

....

....

....

....

....

PRAY:

Jesus, I praise You for indwelling me with the Holy Spirit when I believed in You and confessed that You are the Christ, the Son of the living God. Because of the Spirit, I can dwell, endure, and remain here, in the calling of motherhood. I pray for fruit that lasts in my life and my children's lives.

A RESURRECTED HEART

Read Hebrews 13

KEY VERSE:

He has said, "I will never [under any circumstances] desert you [nor give you up nor leave you without support, nor will I in any degree leave you helpless], nor will I forsake or let you down or relax My hold on you [assuredly not]!"

HEBREWS 13:5 AMP

UNDERSTAND:

Are you in the middle of a painful season (perhaps a friend betrayed you, or you have been diagnosed with a severe illness)?

....

....

....

....

....

....

What are some things hurting your heart in this situation? Journal about your regrets, desires, fears, and doubts.

....

....

....

....

....

....

APPLY:

Scripture tells us that God will never, ever leave us and that no one can snatch us out of His hand when we believe in Jesus (John 10:28). With His help, we can find the grace to move out of our pain into the light—whether the pain comes from the consequences of our own sin, another's choices, or random circumstances.

As we walk with Him, we begin to see that, in fact, God *Himself* is the light that leads us through the darkness. We don't have to live in the darkness of sin, fear, or bitterness. We can turn our face toward the light of His grace and face the very things that are causing us grief—because we're not alone.

Just as Jesus resurrected Lazarus from a physical death, He can rescue us from spiritual and emotional turmoil. Trust in this fact: Our Savior can resurrect your heart. More than that, He longs to do so.

PRAY:

I need a renewed heart, Father God. Life has battered and bruised me, and I want to leave anger and bitterness behind. Show me Your goodness once again and restore my joy through the light of Your presence. Thank You for never leaving or forsaking me. May my children also see the reality of Your presence and praise You.

GOD SEES YOU

Read Genesis 16

KEY VERSE:

She gave this name to the LORD who spoke to her: "You are the God who sees me," for she said, "I have now seen the One who sees me."

GENESIS 16:13 NIV

UNDERSTAND:

In what ways do you feel unseen or overlooked as a mom?

How does it make you feel to know God sees you? Do you truly believe He does? Why or why not?

APPLY:

Hagar was property, a person whose job was to serve Abraham and Sarah. This slave woman had no rights or freedom of her own. And yet God saw Hagar. (Her story occurs in Genesis 16 and 21 and is a fascinating read.)

God met her in the wilderness—twice—and gave Hagar a magnificent promise, especially for a slave woman. She praised "the One" who met her in the desert, and she ended up being the only woman in scripture to give God a name: *El Roi*, or "The God who sees me."

We are seen just as Hagar was, no matter how invisible, taken for granted, or overlooked we feel. We are loved by an all-powerful, all-knowing, all-merciful God. No matter our pasts, our status, our circumstances, or how dry and lonely the wilderness is, God is with us and for us. He showed on the cross that He loves us more than we can even comprehend.

Take those truths to heart and be encouraged.

....

....

....

....

....

....

....

....

....

PRAY:

Thank You, most Holy God, that You see me and love me. What a difference it makes to know I am seen by You even in my most lonely moments. I praise You for Your presence and peace. Help me to see You more clearly and love You more fervently.

SINK DOWN INTO HIS GRACE

Read Psalm 46

KEY VERSE:

"Be still, and know that I am God."

PSALM 46:10 NIV

UNDERSTAND:

Do you think of God as someone to relax around or someone to perform for? (Be honest.) Why do you think that is?

....

....

....

....

....

....

How might your children see God based on your answer above? How could you encourage them to see Him as loving and forgiving?

....

....

....

....

....

....

....

APPLY:

Small children love "hidey holes." They crawl into cupboards, make nests in closets, and even wedge themselves into boxes. It seems kids are comforted by being surrounded on every side by solidity.

In today's key verse, the Hebrew word *raphah* is translated "be still." It has many meanings, among them "relax" and "sink down." Have you ever thought of God as someone to relax into?

Many of us grow up with distorted views of our heavenly Father, due to the imperfect parenting and religious teaching we received. We think of God as a stern father who is constantly disappointed by our feeble efforts to obey.

Jesus taught instead that God is a tender, faithful Shepherd who is ready to lay down His life for His sheep. He's a safe place to run to and a solid place to sink down into. Today, crawl like a child into your Father's lap and relax into His grace. Talk to Him as a friend and find comfort in His arms.

....

....

....

....

....

....

....

....

....

PRAY:

I long to know You as a safe place to run to, God,
instead of fearing that You will be disappointed in me.
Give me a proper view of Your character. Thank You that I
can relax and sink down into Your arms. What a gift!

THE GIFT OF GRACE

Read Isaiah 41

KEY VERSE:

"For I am the Lord your God who takes hold of your right hand and says to you, Do not fear; I will help you."

Isaiah 41:13 NIV

UNDERSTAND:

In what areas do you struggle with mom guilt?

....

....

....

....

Would you call yourself a perfectionist? Why or why not?

....

....

....

....

Think of several ways in which you regularly sacrifice and demonstrate love for your children. Write them all down.

....

....

....

....

....

APPLY:

Whether you're a mother of littles or teens, your energy is affected by lack of sleep and the kids' seemingly boundless energy or schedules. It's easy to feel guilty about undone housework or dirty hair (yours or the children's). In this age of experts who tout the best way to do just about anything, it's difficult to find and maintain your own rhythm as a mom. The constant barrage of information—and people jumping online to state their opinions—about nursing, sleep training, school choice, and other topics fans the flame of mom guilt. Many moms spend way too much time beating themselves up about dirty floors. The cure? Learn to give yourself grace. Your children know they are loved, and they will remember fun family conversations much more than whether or not those talks were held over plates of fast food. Your house might not be spotless, but it can be peaceful and full of laughter.

....

....

....

....

....

....

....

....

....

....

PRAY:

Thank You that I don't have to be perfect; I just need to be surrendered daily to You. I know You are perfect, Lord, and You can fill in the gaps where I am weak and human. Help me to do my best as a mom and leave the results to You.

HE SEES IT ALL

Read Matthew 6

KEY VERSE:

"So that your giving may be in secret.
And your Father who sees in secret will reward you."
Matthew 6:4 ESV

UNDERSTAND:

What parenting challenges are you facing right now? Do you feel uplifted, delighted in, and cheered on by your heavenly Father in those difficulties?

When you feel unprepared and overwhelmed, reread Matthew 6:4. Then print it out and put it somewhere you can see it the next time you need encouragement.

APPLY:

We moms recognize that in the big scheme of things, potty training, curfew squabbles, and sibling battles are not world-shattering events. We've also heard that one day we'll look back on this time in our lives with nostalgia, asking, "why did they have to grow up so fast?" Still, maintaining momentum and motivation in the mundane is difficult.

Friend, let this encourage you: Even the smallest, way-out-of-the-spotlight details of our days matter to Him—whether we're teaching young brothers to resolve conflict themselves or sticking to our boundaries with a teen daughter. God has placed us in the ministry of motherhood to invest in their lives and impart the love of God. Each moment we give of ourselves, we make deposits into their future.

We train them up to let them go, praying they seek Him first as they fly. Trust that God is providing; not only that, but He also cheers you on as you parent your child(ren).

PRAY:

God, my days are filled with the mundane, and it's hard to be motivated. I feel frustrated by the methodical march of motherhood. Help me see it with eternal eyes, as a ministry. Thank You for providing wisdom, patience, and most of all, Your presence.

END THE COMPARISON TRAP

Read 2 Corinthians 10

KEY VERSE:

Oh, don't worry; we wouldn't dare say that we are as wonderful as these other men who tell you how important they are! But they are only comparing themselves with each other, using themselves as the standard of measurement. How ignorant!

2 CORINTHIANS 10:12 NLT

UNDERSTAND:

Do you compare your family to other families? Does that make you feel "less than" or more important? How might that habit be harming you?

....

....

....

....

....

How might it change your expectations, thoughts, and emotions if you let go of the need to compare?

....

....

....

....

....

....

APPLY:

While motherhood is not a competitive sport, we moms are champions at comparing ourselves to others and measuring our kids against impossible standards. We want our children to be successful in everything they touch, and we want ours to be the gold standard of parenting.

We can read all the "right" parenting books, listen to experts, and decide that we will never yell, criticize, or use television as a babysitter. Still, it only takes giving birth to show us the folly of our resolutions.

There's nothing wrong with wanting the best for our families. But we need to remember that we're only human, and our kids are too. In addition, the world's standards should not be the ruler by which we measure anything—especially ourselves or our children.

Learn to let go of human measurement and comparing your family to others. Instead, make Jesus and a gospel-centered life the only gold standard.

....

....

....

....

....

....

....

....

....

PRAY:

Heavenly Father, forgive me for comparing myself and my family to others. I thank and praise You that the standards You set for me are met in the person of Jesus. How freeing that is! Help me to let go of human measurements and unrealistic expectations. May my family live gospel-centered lives that show the world who You are.

GOD PROTECTS HIS REPUTATION

Read Psalm 23

KEY VERSE:

He restores my strength. He leads me down the right paths for the sake of his reputation.

PSALM 23:3 NET

UNDERSTAND:

What does it mean to you that God promises to lead you (and your children) down the right paths?

....

....

....

....

....

....

How does God look out for your family's best interests?

....

....

....

....

....

....

....

APPLY:

In Psalm 23, David—himself a shepherd—used the relationship between a shepherd and his flock to portray truths about our heavenly Father.

Verse 3 reveals why God takes such good care of us: It's who He is. The NET Bible commentary notes that to protect their reputations, "Shepherds, who sometimes hired out their services. . .had to know the 'lay of the land' and make sure they led the sheep down the right paths to the proper destinations. The underlying reality is a profound theological truth: God must look out for the best interests of the one He has promised to protect because if He fails to do so, His faithfulness could legitimately be called into question and His reputation damaged."

Friend, whatever you're up against, God's faithfulness will not allow Him to fail you. He doesn't need a PR firm, because He is consistent and perfect in His love for us. When we're feeling pummeled by life, we can take comfort in that truth.

....

....

....

....

....

....

....

....

....

PRAY:

Lord, I'm grateful that You continually provide so well for me and my family. Your goodness and mercy follow us. Today, I feel pummeled by circumstances and need Your shepherding care as I shepherd my children. Thank You that You take care of me for Your name's sake.

ENCOURAGE FAMILY FAITH CONVERSATIONS

Read Psalm 145

KEY VERSE:

One generation shall praise Your works to another, and shall declare Your mighty acts.

PSALM 145:4 NKJV

UNDERSTAND:

Write down several ways God has answered both large and small prayers in the last year.

....

....

....

Write a plan to share those blessings with your children this week.

....

....

....

Think of a creative way your family could keep track of answered prayers over the next few months (index card file, dry-erase board, jar with slips of paper, etc.)

....

....

....

....

APPLY:

Have you seen God answer a prayer lately? Tell your children about it. Did He provide financially in an unexpected way recently? Talk about it at the dinner table with your family. Do you have a story from your extended family of faith restored, lives changed, or forgiveness shared? Let your teenagers know about it.

Of course, we all have different backgrounds and personalities. Some of us were raised in homes where faith was private or mocked. Others have a painful past and have only recently begun to talk about our relationship with God and how He has sustained or changed us. Still, the more we share God's work and ways in conversation, the more natural it will seem to do so. Eventually, talking about faith can become as regular as breathing.

God's Word encourages us to declare His mighty acts and praise His works across the generations. The next time your relatives (extended or immediate) gather, ask questions that might lead to faith conversations. When your children have their own families, they will find it a natural part of life.

....

....

....

....

....

....

....

....

PRAY:

You are such a faithful Father! I praise You for all the things You do and are. Help me to be bold in sharing Your works of grace with my children and relatives. Give me creativity to find ways to keep track of all Your answers to the many prayers we pray.

PRAY ALWAYS

Read 1 Thessalonians 5

KEY VERSES:

Rejoice always, pray without ceasing, give thanks in all circumstances; for this is the will of God in Christ Jesus for you.
1 THESSALONIANS 5:16–18 ESV

UNDERSTAND:

Which of your worries feel too small to pray about? Why do you think you believe some needs are trivial to God?

....

....

....

....

....

....

Ask God for ideas on how to incorporate more prayer, about both small and large things, into daily life with your family.

....

....

....

....

....

....

....

APPLY:

Have you ever thought a concern was too trivial to "bother" God about? Perhaps your child was having night terrors or your husband needed a friend. Maybe you're worried about an upcoming decision or paying a bill, and you think, *In the scheme of the world's problems, this is small.*

The Greek phrase translated "at all times" or "without ceasing" is *en panti kario*. It conveys the idea that every detail, down to the smallest notion, is included.

Not only can we go to God with everything that burdens us, we can also teach our children to do the same. For example, the next time you're driving around doing errands and see an ambulance, pray out loud with your children for the paramedics and people they're treating. Notice a police car with sirens blaring? Pray for the officers in the car and those they are speeding toward. Eventually, prayer will become second nature.

....

....

....

....

....

....

....

....

....

PRAY:

Thank You for being concerned with everything that burdens me, Father. Give me creativity and perseverance as I learn to pray continually. I want to involve my children in praying for even the smallest details so that we can learn the habit of prayer.

HE GIVES PERFECT SHALOM

Read Isaiah 26

KEY VERSE:

You will keep the mind that is dependent on You in perfect peace, for it is trusting in You.

Isaiah 26:3 HCSB

UNDERSTAND:

What area is hardest for you to surrender to God: your thoughts, plans, or schedule? Why?

What is your first instinct when you feel panicked—prayer or problem-solving? What should it be? How can you remind yourself to go to God first?

APPLY:

Motherhood is a marathon, not a sprint. Day by day, we parent the children God has given us, guiding them through a myriad of circumstances. At times the chaos of life threatens to steal our peace, and we falter. Instead of going to God in prayer, we ask Facebook friends for input or try to fix a situation ourselves.

Today's key verse gives us the answer for finding and holding on to peace (the lasting kind God alone gives): dependence on Him. The Hebrew word here translated as "peace" is *shalom*. Shalom encompasses not just an absence of conflict but also a complete wholeness in every area of a nation's or person's being. It's that ideal that is translated "perfect peace."

Don't you want that kind of wholeness in yourself and your family? If so, surrender today—and every day—your thoughts, plans, and schedule to the Father who longs to grant *shalom* to you.

....

....

....

....

....

....

....

....

....

....

PRAY:

Abba Father, I confess I often try to fix things instead of running to You. Remind me to lay down chaos management and pick up prayer and Your Word on the days I get overwhelmed. I long for shalom in my heart and home, and I praise You in advance for that gift.

HE GENTLY LEADS

Read Isaiah 40

KEY VERSE:

He tends his flock like a shepherd: He gathers the lambs in his arms and carries them close to his heart; he gently leads those that have young.

Isaiah 40:11 NIV

UNDERSTAND:

Do you ever feel frightened by the responsibility of motherhood? If so, what gives you the most fear?

How does the image the prophet Isaiah gives in today's key verse speak to you? Do you see God as a tender shepherd? What might it mean to your parenting if you concentrated on this image of His care for you and your children?

APPLY:

Parenthood is an immense responsibility, one that can take our breath away. In fact, if we think about the current state of world affairs and how much we need to teach our children before they leave our homes and start their own lives, we can quickly move into panic mode.

Thankfully, God doesn't leave us on our own to figure things out or write us off when we mess up. Instead, He treats us kindly and with mercy, holding us close to His heart when we feel overwhelmed and leading us through minefields and valleys alike. And even when we make mistakes, He promises to guide and love our children through their own journeys.

Note that God is seen as a tender shepherd in today's key verse. He is also portrayed as a leader and guide. Unlike the religious and political leaders who had guided the Israelites to ruin and captivity, their Lord and Shepherd was trustworthy.

He still is.

....

....

....

....

....

....

....

....

....

PRAY:

Gentle Shepherd, thank You for leading me with mercy and grace. I want to follow You closely and listen to Your voice intently so that You can guide me through every situation I come up against. Give me ears to hear Your voice and a soul attuned to Your Spirit.

STORE UP MOMENTS

Read Luke 2

KEY VERSE:

But Mary was treasuring up all these things in her heart and meditating on them.

LUKE 2:19 HCSB

UNDERSTAND:

Are you impatient for your child to reach milestones? Why or why not?

Find a way to record funny, exceptional, and normal moments—on your phone, on a computer, or in a journal—so you can look back on them one day.

APPLY:

It's hard not to "run ahead" in motherhood, especially with a first child. When he has long crying jags in the middle of the night, we want him to hurry and grow so we can finally sleep again. While she's in diapers, we're impatient for her to be potty-trained. And on it goes.

One of the best (and also hardest) things we can do as moms is to live in the moment and not get caught up in thoughts of "if only. . ." or "when this happens, I will. . ." Though it's difficult and exhausting to parent an infant, the stage does pass; and they begin to crawl, walk, and even run.

Take it from older moms: Try to treasure moments and store them in your mind. Better yet, take notes so you can go back and read the highlights you share with your family. Those notes will become treasures when your children eventually leave the nest and fly away.

....

....

....

....

....

....

....

....

....

....

....

PRAY:

Forgive me, Lord, for not living in the moment. I want to fully engage in my life, finding contentment and peace in the present. I've heard it said that the "days are long, but the years are short." Keep me centered in You, Lord, so I can store up the treasures that come my way.

LEAVE IT AT THE ALTAR

Read 1 Samuel 1

KEY VERSE:

[Hannah] said, "May your servant find favor in your eyes." Then she went her way and ate something, and her face was no longer downcast.

1 Samuel 1:18 NIV

UNDERSTAND:

What emotions do you have when someone hurts you? What about when someone mistreats your child?

How might Hannah's example encourage you? List some actions you could take next time you (or a family member) are wounded.

APPLY:

God made moms to be protective. We may appear mild-mannered, but cross one of our children, and we go into "mama bear" mode.

The biblical mother Hannah serves as an example for us of how to react when someone hurts us or our kids. In today's verse, Hannah didn't yet have an answer to her request (the happy ending comes later), but she trusted the Lord enough to leave her problems at His feet.

Do we say we believe in God's goodness but harbor fear of surrendering the other person (and our wounds) completely to Him? How much simpler our lives would be if we followed Hannah's example and left our problems at the altar. She refused to worry herself sick, and she didn't take revenge on her rival. She knew God had her best interests at heart and that He would deal out justice to her enemies—in His own way and time.

PRAY:

In my humanness, I want to strike back when someone mistreats me or a family member. Help me to bring my wounded heart to You, Father, and give me the grace not to seek retaliation. Instead, impart Your strength so I can surrender my hurts in Your presence.

TAKE UP YOUR SHIELD

Read Ephesians 6

KEY VERSES:

Therefore put on the full armor of God, so that when the day of evil comes, you may be able to stand your ground, and after you have done everything, to stand. Stand firm then, with the belt of truth buckled around your waist, with the breastplate of righteousness in place, and with your feet fitted with the readiness that comes from the gospel of peace. In addition to all this, take up the shield of faith, with which you can extinguish all the flaming arrows of the evil one.

EPHESIANS 6:13–16 NIV

UNDERSTAND:

What do you think of when you read the word *shield*? What purposes does a shield serve in battle?

....

....

....

....

....

Satan's weapons are many and varied. List a few of his tactics. How can you protect yourself against them?

....

....

....

....

....

APPLY:

The Greek word Paul used for shield is *thureos*, from a root word that means door or gate. During the days of the early church, a Roman soldier's shield was an oblong as large as a door; it completely covered the soldier wielding it. Roman soldiers' shields were woven from leather strips. Every morning, they oiled their shield. If it wasn't oiled, the strips on the shield would become brittle and thus vulnerable to an opponent's spear.

We believe in a God who is far bigger than any weapons of fear or distraction the enemy can hurl at us. We can be sure He can handle any circumstance we will ever face. But even as busy moms, we need to daily oil our shield of faith (just like you're doing by reading this book and studying the Bible). As we do, we learn more about Him. The better we know Him, the more we can trust Him.

....

....

....

....

....

....

....

....

....

....

....

PRAY:

Lord, forgive me for the times I don't seek Your truth. Help me to "oil" my shield of faith daily by trusting in Your Word. Give me faith that wins out over fear, moves mountains of doubt, and causes the enemy to flee. Thank You for the spiritual armor You provide.

SHINE LIKE THE STARS

Read Philippians 2

KEY VERSES:

Do everything without grumbling and arguing, so that you may be blameless and pure, children of God who are faultless in a crooked and perverted generation, among whom you shine like stars in the world. Hold firmly to the message of life. Then I can boast in the day of Christ that I didn't run or labor for nothing.

PHILIPPIANS 2:14–16 HCSB

UNDERSTAND:

What are you tempted to complain or argue about?

Which attribute of our heavenly Father are you most grateful for: perfection, purity, mercy, goodness, patience, life-giver. . . ?

APPLY:

In Philippians 2, Paul encouraged the church at Philippi not to complain or argue and to hold firmly to the Word of God. Jesus is known as "the Word made flesh." When we hold on to Him, we become blameless and pure—by *His* grace and mercy and not by our efforts. Then we can be a shining light in a dark world.

In a me-first culture, the Father wants us to seek His will and approval, not the wealth or fame others desire. And though we stumble and fall regularly, our heavenly Father is immeasurably good to us. Like a master craftsman, He gently hones and perfects our rough edges. His goal is to make us more like Jesus; and He is a patient, loving artist who sees the women we were created to be and isn't content until we're fully transformed.

Pray for God to sculpt You into a closer likeness of Jesus each day.

....

....

....

....

....

....

....

....

....

....

....

PRAY:

Heavenly Father, thank You for the gift of Jesus. Through His life, death, and resurrection, I stand blameless and pure before You. Forgive me when I complain or argue, and help me seek Your approval, not the world's. Make me more like You.

REJECT PERFECTIONISM

Read Matthew 5

KEY VERSE:

"You, therefore, will be perfect [growing into spiritual maturity both in mind and character, actively integrating godly values into your daily life], as your heavenly Father is perfect."

MATTHEW 5:48 AMP

UNDERSTAND:

Do you struggle with perfectionism? If so, in what areas?

How do you react when your kids make mistakes and disobey? Why do you think you respond that way?

APPLY:

Are you a perfectionist? Many moms are. Would it comfort you to know that in today's key verse the word *perfect* can also be translated as *mature*? The only perfect person who ever walked the earth was Jesus, and though we desire to be like Him, we are human and will stumble and fall.

Part of becoming mature means learning that we—and our children—have limits. We have just one life, and our Savior died and rose again so that it could be abundant, or filled with purpose, contentment, and peace. As busy moms, we can experience abundant life daily if we reject the lie of perfectionism, recognize our limits, and reorient our lives daily around Jesus.

When we remember that Jesus loved us enough to leave the perfection of heaven and dirty His feet with the soil of earth, we can see ourselves as He does. We can accept God's mercy and impart that mercy to the imperfect people around us.

PRAY:

Jesus, You left heaven to reconcile us to God. Your perfect life and obedience made my relationship with our Father possible. I can never thank You enough! As You give me mercy for my faults and sins, help me impart mercy to my family and others.

HE FIGHTS FOR YOU

Read Exodus 14

KEY VERSES:

Moses answered the people, "Do not be afraid. Stand firm and you will see the deliverance the LORD will bring you today. The Egyptians you see today you will never see again. The LORD will fight for you; you need only to be still."

EXODUS 14:13–14 NIV

UNDERSTAND:

What is the biggest concern facing you or your family right now? Spend some time in prayer about it.

....

....

....

....

....

How do you think the Israelites felt when they were staring at the Red Sea with the Egyptians closing in on them? How do you think they felt both during and after God moved so mightily on their behalf?

....

....

....

....

....

....

APPLY:

The Israelites' enemies were in fierce pursuit, and in front of God's chosen ones stood an enormous expanse of water. They were petrified and cried to Moses for salvation. But God, not Moses, fought for the Israelites—as He fights for us today. They needed only to wait and watch.

Mom, what feels like an uncrossable ocean in your life? Is it a discipline problem with a child, troubling marriage issue, or worrisome debt? We want to rush in, attempting to fix the problem ourselves. Next time you're faced with what seems like an impossible situation, pray and seek God's wisdom.

Then—as hard as it is to do so—be still until you are sure of what He wants you to do next. God will make sure you arrive on dry land, and in doing so, He may slay a few of those enemies you've been running from.

....

....

....

....

....

....

....

....

....

....

PRAY:

I relate to the Israelites sometimes, Lord. I see an obstacle in front of me, and I tremble with fear. However, I know You are powerful and can deliver me from what terrifies and perplexes me. Give me the patience and courage to be still and let You work in my life.

WAIT IN EXPECTANT HOPE

Read Hebrews 6

KEY VERSES:

In the same way God wanted to demonstrate more clearly to the heirs of the promise that his purpose was unchangeable, and so he intervened with an oath, so that we who have found refuge in him may find strong encouragement to hold fast to the hope set before us through two unchangeable things, since it is impossible for God to lie. We have this hope as an anchor for the soul, sure and steadfast, which reaches inside behind the curtain, where Jesus our forerunner entered on our behalf.

HEBREWS 6:17–20 NET

UNDERSTAND:

What reasons do we as believers have for a sure and steadfast hope?

....

....

....

....

In what areas in your life do you need hope the most? Pray about them.

....

....

....

....

....

APPLY:

Our world groans from political division, wars, and disasters; we slog through financial and familial stress, job changes, and health crises; and our children face temptations we never could have imagined.

We need hope. In the Old Testament, *hope* is often translated from the Hebrew word *yachal,* meaning "trust." In the New Testament, the word used for *hope* is *elpis,* which can be translated "to expect or anticipate with pleasure."

Therefore, hope in the biblical sense equals trust and faith, an expectation of good things. One mom's young child used to pray using the phrase "God, I hope the dog gets well. I hope Nana comes to visit." She wondered whether she should correct him. But when she found out the biblical meanings of the word *hope*, she decided her son had innocently been praying with wisdom. He simply trusted God and expected good things when he prayed. We can learn from his innocent, complete trust.

....

....

....

....

....

....

....

....

....

PRAY:

Father, You are my hope and peace. Comfort me with Your presence and Word. Let me not neglect it, or You, when I'm afraid, but instead run to You with an open mind and heart. As I do, give me assurance that You are still at work in this world.

TRUST GOD'S PLAN

Read Proverbs 16

KEY VERSE:

We can make our plans, but the Lord determines our steps.

Proverbs 16:9 NLT

UNDERSTAND:

Do you have difficulty trusting the Lord's plan for your children?

Do you ever struggle with trying to solve or "fix" their problems yourself?

APPLY:

Even when we trust God with our own problems and concerns, it's difficult for moms to trust God when it comes to our children. That's another level of surrender!

One mom of several sons admitted, "Often I find myself struggling when God's plan for my life looks different than I thought it would. When my older children were young, I never really felt successful at moderating their sibling rivalry and bickering. I had lots of self-condemnation because I felt like I should be able to referee their squabbles in a satisfactory manner. However, I learned a very valuable lesson—that children must work some things out for themselves. My adult children seem to have learned this, thankfully. It was the Lord who taught them and not me! I feel like I tried to solve all their problems, and that is never the Lord's plan."

How might the Lord want you to trust Him with your children's lives today?

....

....

....

....

....

....

....

....

....

PRAY:

Creator God, as much as I'd like to, I know it wouldn't be good for my family if I could fix everything. Help me to pray and surrender all the things that concern us. I know You determine our steps, and You are faithful in everything You plan. May Your purposes prevail in our home.

SAY GOODBYE TO MOM GUILT

Read Romans 8

KEY VERSES:

And we know that in all things God works for the good of those who love him, who have been called according to his purpose. For those God foreknew he also predestined to be conformed to the image of his Son, that he might be the firstborn among many brothers and sisters.

ROMANS 8:28–29 NIV

UNDERSTAND:

In what areas of motherhood do you struggle with guilt? Why do you think those areas bring up guilty emotions?

....

....

....

....

....

Do you believe God works all things together for good like today's verse says? If so, how could this bring comfort when you feel guilty?

....

....

....

....

....

....

APPLY:

Mom guilt can be almost debilitating. From the moment we decide whether to nurse or bottle-feed, we feel guilty for what our children eat or don't eat, consume on television or social media, and much more. But God doesn't want us to live under a cloud of guilt!

One mother says, "My husband and I had a baby after our older children were grown. He's such a blessing to us but is being raised virtually as an only child (with parents who are more tired than they used to be). There's a constant balance of reminding him he's in a unique situation—one that the Lord chose specifically for him. I can get caught up in guilt, but when I slow down enough to remember how much God loves us and is always working all things for our good, I can rest in His plan. I can trust Him to bring about things in ways I never would have thought of."

PRAY:

You are a faithful Father. I believe You are in control and are working every situation—the lovely and the difficult—for my good and my loved ones' good, according to Your divine purpose. Help me rest in Your plan and trust You more every day.

HE IS ALL WE NEED

Read Psalm 73

KEY VERSE:

But as for me, God's presence is all I need.
I have made the Sovereign LORD my shelter,
as I declare all the things you have done.
PSALM 73:28 NET

UNDERSTAND:

What is the number one thing or person you depend on? Whose presence calms you down and helps you endure a difficult time?

Think about what your husband or children would say to the above question if they were asked about who you depend on. Would their honest response be different from yours? Why or why not?

APPLY:

It's easy to skim over today's verse (and similar scriptures), not letting it sink down into our hearts. Instead, stop and ask yourself: *Is God's presence really all I need? Is it my daily sustenance, or am I distracted and distressed by circumstances both personal and global?*

When we daily put our trust fully in God, we spend life more aware of His abundant blessings in our lives. We find ourselves thanking Him more and asking for less, because we are childlike in our dependence on the one who provides everything. In addition, our loved ones notice and partake in our joy when we put away worry and put on praise.

As renowned preacher and scholar Matthew Henry noted in his commentary on Psalm 73:28, "Let us trust in the Lord, that we may declare all his works. . . . Those that with an upright heart put their trust in God shall never want matter for thanksgiving to him."

....

....

....

....

....

....

....

....

....

....

PRAY:

My thoughts are easily distracted and overwhelmed, Lord, but I know You are trustworthy and have provided me with all I need. Give me the stillness of mind that comes from fully trusting in You. I want to be wrapped up in thanksgiving that overflows whenever I think or talk about You.

GOD'S RIGHT HAND

Read Isaiah 41

KEY VERSE:

"So do not fear, for I am with you; do not be dismayed,
for I am your God. I will strengthen you and help you;
I will uphold you with my righteous right hand."

Isaiah 41:10 NIV

UNDERSTAND:

Do you ever worry about making the wrong decision? What was the last choice you felt torn about?

....

....

....

....

....

....

How would it make you feel as a traveler to follow someone who couldn't make a wrong turn?

....

....

....

....

....

....

....

APPLY:

We moms make dozens of small decisions for our families daily. However, the big choices—which town to live in or how to discipline a wayward teen—can loom so large they frighten us. We pray and seek advice, but we may also feel paralyzed with fear, believing the wrong move will doom us to a second-class life.

Here's the truth: God's righteous right hand, as noted in today's verse, can be trusted to do what is right in every situation. Unlike us, He never makes a wrong turn. What a truly comforting thought!

Because Christ lives in us, we don't need to fear taking the wrong path. Jesus gave the Holy Spirit to help and strengthen us, upholding us on our journey. He can also redeem our mistakes and correct our course. Are you facing a difficult decision? Know that He is with you and there is no reason for dismay.

PRAY:

Holy Spirit, You are a trustworthy guide. I praise You because You do the right thing in every circumstance; therefore, I don't need to fear making a bad choice. Instead, I ask for Your wisdom and discernment. Make the path forward clear, and when I step in the wrong direction, correct me.

SEEK GOD'S APPROVAL

Read Galatians 1

KEY VERSE:

Obviously, I'm not trying to win the approval of people, but of God. If pleasing people were my goal, I would not be Christ's servant.

GALATIANS 1:10 NLT

UNDERSTAND:

Have you ever been shunned or ridiculed for your belief in Jesus?

What does loyalty mean to you?

Whose approval matters to you? Whom do you seek to please?

APPLY:

Who has your loyalty? Your husband, a coffee shop, a department store, your girlfriends?

Loyalty is an admirable trait, but our ultimate fidelity should be to Christ. In a culture whose definitions of truth are ever changing, we are called to stand boldly for Jesus instead of being afraid of those who would reject us for our biblical beliefs.

In his letter to the church in Galatia, the apostle Paul rebuked some of the believers because they were believing a false gospel. He was unapologetically bold in the face of those who would twist the truth for their own or others' benefit. Paul was ready to die for the faith he had once himself (as a proud Pharisee named Saul) rejected and persecuted.

Which will you be: a mother who seeks to please other people, or a mom who holds God's approval as the highest standard? Remember that people are fickle and their opinions change, but God never changes. He will help you stand firm.

....

....

....

....

....

....

....

....

PRAY:

If I'm honest, Father, I care too much what people think of me.
Help me to center my heart around Your approval alone.
Give me courage to stand for Your truth in a world of
changing standards and definitions. May my children and I
never bow to idols of this world but instead bow only to You.

CURBING RECKLESS WORDS

Read Proverbs 12

KEY VERSE:

Speaking recklessly is like the thrusts of a sword,
but the words of the wise bring healing.
PROVERBS 12:18 NET

UNDERSTAND:

When are you most likely to speak harshly to your child(ren)?

....

....

....

Think of a time when you regretted the words you spoke recklessly. How did you handle the situation—immediately apologize and ask for forgiveness, ignore the hurtful words, or go back to the child later in contrition?

....

....

....

How do you think God would want you to handle such a situation next time?

....

....

....

....

APPLY:

We've all been there. A child talks back to us, and we snap at them with harsh words. Suddenly, their eyes widen in shock and fill with tears. We've hurt them, and regret fills our thoughts as we try to make amends.

No mother is patient, kind, and gentle all the time. So how do we prevent speaking recklessly and instead speak wisely—even when we're not having a good day?

First, we can't do it on our own. Self-control is listed in Galatians 6 as a fruit of the Spirit, which means we grow in that discipline as we grow in Christ. Second, we won't develop control of our tongues overnight. Like any spiritual growth, it happens daily as we read the Word, surrender our thoughts and attitudes, and pray for Christlikeness.

Finally, know that we will continue to mess up because we're human. When we do, let's model humility and confession to our kids.

....

....

....

....

....

....

....

....

....

....

PRAY:

Jesus, in my own strength, I lack self-control. Help me to spend time with You daily so I can grow in Christlikeness. Forgive me for the times I lose my temper and hurt my loved ones. Grant me the humility to apologize and seek forgiveness when I sin by speaking recklessly.

JESUS, OUR REASON FOR HOPE

Read Colossians 1

KEY VERSE:

To them God has chosen to make known among the Gentiles the glorious riches of this mystery, which is Christ in you, the hope of glory.

COLOSSIANS 1:27 NIV

UNDERSTAND:

What circumstances cause you to feel hopeless or full of doubt and fear?

....

....

....

Do you pray when you don't feel like it? Remember, God hears those prayers that are prayed in the middle of difficult times as well as those we pray in celebration.

....

....

....

Think about Jesus' followers after His crucifixion and before His resurrection. What do you imagine they felt and thought?

....

....

....

....

APPLY:

Sometimes life's uncertainty and unexpected losses steal our joy. Maybe today the dark and doubt from grief and confusion are weighing you down. You feel weak, weary, and worried. You see no way that things could turn around, and you're tired of praying. It hurts to hope because life feels cruel and indifferent.

Perhaps you relate to the men and women who hid in fear and sorrow after Jesus was crucified. While we know the Resurrection changed everything, they were grieving and afraid of being hunted down and killed too.

Ironically, when faith feels impossible, that's when it's most needed. God asks us to trust in the dark. It's not easy, but when we pray with even a shred of faith, He moves. Our heavenly Father turns our persistent pleading into peace when we don't let feelings rule but instead stand firm in the truth of God's Word. We can have hope because He is our hope and dwells inside of us.

....

....

....

....

....

....

....

....

....

PRAY:

Father, remind my heart that miracles are Your specialty. No matter how hopeless my situation looks, I choose to believe that You are good, loving, and faithful. I know that Jesus' resurrection is the reason I can hope and the reason I can share that hope with others.

WALK WITH INTEGRITY

Read Proverbs 20

KEY VERSE:

The godly walk with integrity;
blessed are their children who follow them.
PROVERBS 20:7 NLT

UNDERSTAND:

What does the word *integrity* mean to you? Is there someone in your circle you picture when you hear that word? What made you think of them?

....

....

....

Are there areas in which you struggle to live completely honestly and obediently?

....

....

....

....

Why does scripture promise our children will be blessed if we walk with integrity?

....

....

....

....

APPLY:

A life of godliness happens choice by daily choice. While we often think about integrity as something leaders need, we moms are leaders in our homes as well as our communities, churches, and workplaces. We model Christlike character when we honor truth in small moments. We live with integrity at the dinner table when we refuse to tell white lies, in our car while obeying traffic laws, and in our relationship with our husband when we choose not to flirt with a handsome neighbor.

Our children take in much more than we realize, and they are watching us. As you've probably heard, "much more is caught than taught." When we refuse to take the easy path of least resistance—steal a few office supplies to use at home, cheat a bit on our taxes to get a bigger refund—our kids may notice. Let's make sure the actions they see us take are in line with what we teach them.

....

....

....

....

....

....

....

....

....

....

....

PRAY:

Father, I long for my family to see me as a woman of godly character, one who doesn't take the easy path but who chooses obedience over ease. Give me the kind of heart that honors You above all else so my family may be blessed because of how I live.

THE KEY TO LASTING PEACE

Read Philippians 4

KEY VERSES:

Don't worry about anything; instead, pray about everything. Tell God what you need, and thank him for all he has done. Then you will experience God's peace, which exceeds anything we can understand. His peace will guard your hearts and minds as you live in Christ Jesus.

PHILIPPIANS 4:6–7 NLT

UNDERSTAND:

Who's the most peaceful person you know? Why do you think they're that way?

....

....

....

....

What worries keep you up at night? Write them down. Now, one by one, pray about them, mentally giving them over to your Father who loves you, and ask God to give you His peace in exchange. Then thank God for His promises and provision.

....

....

....

....

....

APPLY:

Has a health emergency rattled your family? Is a child struggling with a learning disability or bullying? Maybe your brood has recently moved across the state, and everyone feels lonely. Whatever situation you find yourself in, know that the peace of God can be yours.

In Philippians 4:6–7, the apostle Paul noted that supernatural peace would guard our hearts and minds when we place our concerns in the capable hands of our heavenly Father. The kind of peace Paul wrote about was not a fleeting, circumstantial peace that a believer can conjure up on his own. Rather, the peace Paul wrote about is a heaven-sent gift from a loving provider, one beyond our limited understanding.

Paul wrote to the church at Philippi as one who had lived through storms, shipwrecks, hunger, beatings, persecution, and imprisonment. Yet God's peace and joy filled him up to overflowing and made him bold to share the life-giving news of the gospel.

....

....

....

....

....

....

....

....

....

PRAY:

Lord, I need the lasting, supernatural peace that comes from Your Spirit. Circumstances have left me feeling vulnerable, and when I look at the world, I get scared for my children and feel overwhelmed. Guard my heart and mind with Your peace so I can overflow with joy and boldness like the apostle Paul.

IT'S AN ABUNDANT LIFE

Read John 10

KEY VERSE:

"The thief comes only to steal and kill and destroy; I have come so that they may have life, and may have it abundantly."
JOHN 10:10 NET

UNDERSTAND:

Do you feel like you have an ordinary life? Why or why not?

When you hear the words "abundant life," what does that mean to you?

Is your life in line with the biblical meaning of *abundant* (see next page)? If not, what might move it there?

APPLY:

Most of us don't think of our lives as abundant, except when we look at our calendars. But an abundant life doesn't mean our refrigerator is full or all our children's wishes are met. *Abundant* comes from the Greek *periossos,* which means "exceeding" or "above and beyond."

Satan tempts us to despair; Jesus gives us the spiritual fruits of hope and peace. Satan tells us we're not worthy and our sins are too grave for God to love us; Jesus rose from the grave after dying for those very sins so we could be eternally in God's presence. Satan tries to steal our joy; Jesus lives in us and imparts His own joy in our lives. Because of His life, we will live forever with our exceedingly gracious God in an extraordinary place.

That abundant life? It's already begun.

PRAY:

I praise You because I will live forever with You in a glorious place. I thank You because my life now has meaning, purpose, and extraordinary promise. I want my life and my loved ones' lives to be far beyond "regular" because of Your perfect plans. Give us Your heart and mind, Jesus.

REST FOR THE WEARY

Read Matthew 11

KEY VERSE:

Then Jesus said, "Come to me, all of you who are weary and carry heavy burdens, and I will give you rest."
MATTHEW 11:28 NLT

UNDERSTAND:

Do you ever think about Jesus getting tired? He did! How might that comfort and encourage you?

....

....

....

....

....

....

In what way(s) are you most weary right now? Ask God to show you the best ways to help curb the weariness and find strength. (You might need to see a doctor, start a light exercise program, cut back on activities, see a counselor, or get more help.)

....

....

....

....

....

....

APPLY:

There's no exhaustion like mom exhaustion. We deal with late nights and interrupted sleep from colicky babies, nursing infants, or out-until-curfew teenagers. We suffer through long days on little sleep with fussy, demanding children. In addition, navigating our family's schedule packed with meetings, activities, and responsibilities creates weariness in even the most energetic of mothers.

Because He was fully human as well as fully divine, Jesus also knew weariness. Throughout His ministry, He felt the burden of religious leaders' hostility, His followers' questions, and a growing number of people who only wanted miracles instead of a relationship with Him.

Knowing His purpose and keeping in close communion with His Father gave our Savior endurance and strength to face even His toughest hours and days. We can find the same enduring strength from knowing our purpose and nestling close to the one who loves us.

Feeling pressed down by your circumstances? Friend, press into Jesus, and He will help you press on.

....

....

....

....

....

....

....

....

....

PRAY:

Lord, I'm tired. I feel overworked and under-rested. Show me ways to give up my need to be constantly on the go and instead make time for stillness and rest. Help me be creative in finding ways to nestle close to You so I can find strength and endurance.

NIGHT SCHOOL WITH GOD

Read Psalm 16

KEY VERSE:

I will praise the Lord, who counsels me;
even at night my heart instructs me.
Psalm 16:7 NIV

UNDERSTAND:

What thoughts come to your mind when your sleep is interrupted or you can't go to sleep?

....

....

....

....

....

....

What might the psalmist have meant when he said, "Even at night my heart instructs me"?

....

....

....

....

....

....

APPLY:

In the previous entry, we noted that being a mother means you'll often survive on little—or interrupted—sleep, for a variety of reasons. Instead of being consistently in knots about your compromised sleep, why not reframe the situation? Moms can choose to see being awake (when they're feeding/changing a baby, waiting up on a teen to come home, or struggling with insomnia) as an opportunity to pray for family, intercede for others, and seek God. After all, He's up all night too.

Warren Wiersbe commented on Psalm 16 that "David's personal fellowship with the Lord was his greatest joy. This was when God instructed and counseled David and told him what to do and how to do it. David even went to 'night school' to learn the will of God. 'Night' is plural, suggesting 'dark nights' or 'night after night' learning from God."

David is a terrific role model in this case; why not follow his lead and go to night school with your Creator?

....

....

....

....

....

....

....

....

....

PRAY:

I need Your help, Father, to keep a calm heart and clear head during these years of motherhood. Remind me to call on You in the night when I'm up with a sick child, waiting for my older kid to get home, or just fretful and anxious. . .and give me guidance on how best to pray.

A GREAT GOD FOR YOUR GREAT NEED

Read Psalm 86

KEY VERSE:

Have mercy on me, O Lord, for I cry out to you all day long.

PSALM 86:3 NET

UNDERSTAND:

In what ways do you feel inadequate as a mom? Have you ever prayed about those areas, asking God to equip and guide you? If not, why? If so, what has been the result?

....

....

....

....

....

Think about David, anointed as king while still a young shepherd boy, fighting Goliath (one of the first of many battles he would have to fight). How was he so brave in the face of such opposition? And how might that courage have served him well later in life?

....

....

....

....

....

....

APPLY:

There's no job quite like mothering, which daily brings us up against our frailty and inadequacies in the face of our family's needs.

Psalm 86 was written by King David, a man who surely often felt inadequate. David had battled a giant while still a boy, lived on the run from a murderous king, and suffered the grave consequences of his own sin. As Israel's king, he must have felt frail and ill-equipped many times. However, he never gave up on honestly pleading with the Lord to guide, give justice, and deal mercifully with his people.

As pastor and author Steven J. Cole says about Psalm 86 on Bible.org, "The psalm is peppered with 15 requests, some of them repetitive, fired at God with a strong sense of urgency. . . . Our great needs should drive us to pray to the great God, who alone can deliver us."

Turn to that great God now, trusting Him to equip and guide you.

....

....

....

....

....

....

....

....

....

....

PRAY:

Honestly, Father, I feel so overwhelmed at times. The needs of my family bring me to the end of myself. However, I know that's a good place to be because it makes me depend on You. Deal mercifully with me and equip and strengthen me for this calling of motherhood.

MOTHERING FOR HIS GLORY

Read 1 Corinthians 10

KEY VERSE:

So whether you eat or drink, or whatever you do, do it all for the glory of God.

1 CORINTHIANS 10:31 NLT

UNDERSTAND:

What are your least and most favorite responsibilities as a mom? Why?

....

....

....

....

....

....

What frustrates you the most about daily chores/housework? How could you reframe the "to-dos" and redeem the time you spend on mindless work more effectively?

....

....

....

....

....

....

APPLY:

From checking homework to paying bills, the tasks on a mom's to-do list seem never-ending. It can be easy to feel grumpy and frustrated by the lack of appreciation from our family members or the sheer collective size of our responsibilities. In addition, cleaning and organizing don't stay done for long; they must be redone at regular intervals. And with little ones underfoot, messes are constant. It can make any mom irritated.

Today, reassess how you go about checking things off your list. Instead of seeing chores as drudgery, you could listen to sermons, praise music, or encouraging podcasts as you work. Other ideas: Keep an audio Bible accessible on your cell phone and listen to scripture as you do errands, cook, or wash dishes; sing scripture songs with your children as you perform daily household tasks together.

In doing so, you will both prevent your own burnout and show your children that work can be a worshipful activity.

PRAY:

Forgive me, Lord, for so often having a negative view of my daily tasks and for becoming angry because my loved ones don't thank me (or even notice what I do). Help me see each chore as an opportunity to praise and pray. In this way, I will influence my children to see their own responsibilities differently.

BE AN INCLUDER

Read Genesis 29

KEY VERSE:

So Jacob served seven years for Rachel, and they seemed to him but a few days because of the love he had for her.

GENESIS 29:20 ESV

UNDERSTAND:

Think back to a rejection you've faced. What emotions did you feel at that time?

If you've healed from that rejection, how and when did the healing come about? If you have not, pray and ask God for clarity on why you are holding on to the pain. Then pray, journal, talk through the rejection with a trusted friend or counselor, and ask God to help you let go and move on.

APPLY:

The Bible gives us pictures of authentic, raw, dysfunctional relationships. In fact, Leah and Rachel's story reads like a reality show.

Interestingly for a shepherd, Rachel's name means "lamb" or "ewe," and she was described as "beautiful" and "well-favored." No wonder Jacob fell hard within seconds of seeing her. In contrast, Leah's name means "wearied," "faint from sickness," or "cow." She was described as having "weary," "weak," or "delicate" eyes, which scholars say means she was less desirable. Genesis 29:30 plainly states that Jacob "loved Rachel more than Leah." (Ouch!)

Rejection stings, no matter when or how it happens. But to be rejected by a man who chose your sister over you? That had to hurt very deeply. Most of us know that pain firsthand, don't we? We've been passed over in favor of someone else—maybe by a boss or friend.

Though the memory is surely painful, know that God will never reject you or your children. Let the wound encourage you to be an includer, and teach your kids to include and not exclude others.

PRAY:

Holy One, thank You for never rejecting me. I know I can come to You in my weakness, shame, guilt, and regret, and You will still wrap me in Your arms of grace. Help me to be that kind of friend and loved one to the people You send my way.

RUN FROM JEALOUSY

Read Genesis 30

KEY VERSE:

When Rachel saw that she was not bearing Jacob any children, she became jealous of her sister. So she said to Jacob, "Give me children, or I'll die!"

GENESIS 30:1 NIV

UNDERSTAND:

The competition between Rachel and Leah was fierce, and they even involved their servants. Have you ever had an unhealthy rivalry with someone (whether they were aware of it or not)? How did that affect you? What might God want to say to you about that?

....

....

....

....

Does social media affect your mindset as you compare your real life to other women's curated feeds? If so, how could you adjust either your mindset or your social media feeds (or both) to help yourself with this struggle? Pray about your use of social media and ask the Holy Spirit to reveal whether it is healthy or not.

....

....

....

....

....

APPLY:

Leah compared herself to Rachel and felt that she came up short, because Jacob loved her sister more. But Rachel compared herself to her sister and felt that she (Rachel) was on the losing end of the equation because Leah was fertile while Rachel was barren.

Too often, we're not content with the gifts God has given us. We feel envious of an acquaintance's good financial fortune or get jealous of a friend's accomplishment instead of being gracious toward them.

Satan knows he can use insecurities and doubts about our worth to tempt us to jealousy, envy, and even self-hatred. He plants menacing thoughts in our heads: *I'll never measure up. I'm worthless. God can't love me. God can't use me.*

But when we succumb to Satan's schemes, we lose sight of who God has created us to be and what He has specifically called us to do. Let's run from jealousy and toward Him, trusting that His plans for us are perfect and that we are worthy because of Jesus—on whom God's approval eternally rests.

....

....

....

....

....

....

....

....

PRAY:

Forgive me, God, for so often being jealous of others. I play the comparison game and begin to envy their jobs, successes, appearances, or possessions. I know You have given me everything I need, and You delight in me just as I am. Help me to fight against Satan's lies by meditating on scripture and letting You speak the truth over me.

GIVING IN FAITH

Read 1 Kings 17

KEY VERSES:

So she went away and did according to the word of Elijah;
and she and he and her household ate for many days.
The bin of flour was not used up, nor did the jar of oil run dry,
according to the word of the LORD which He spoke by Elijah.

1 KINGS 17:15–16 NKJV

UNDERSTAND:

What do you need the Lord to provide for you and your family today?

What connection does generosity have to gratitude? How could you show gratitude and trust in the Lord before He answers your need?

APPLY:

In Elijah's day, widows had few resources. Still, God sent Elijah to the widow at Zarephath so she could provide for him. And later, he was able to bring back her son from the dead. In both cases, Elijah worked miracles—once with a bit of flour and some oil, which God replenished daily, and once by pleading with God to resurrect the widow's boy.

Maybe you're worried today because your family's resources aren't covering your bills. Or perhaps you're grieving a loss, and you see no way God can ever heal your heart. Your joy has left, and all you feel is anguish.

Whatever your need, God has promised to take care of those who trust in Him. Not only that, He also asks us to give to others, like the widow did with Elijah. Ask God to show you where there's a need, and generously give something away—money, food, or another kind of help. Do so in faith that there is always more than enough in God's economy. Who knows what kind of eternal impact your obedience will have?

....

....

....

....

....

....

....

....

PRAY:

Lord, I can get stingy and anxious when I look at my situation, but I want my children to see me as a giver—not a fretter. Forgive me for forgetting that You have always taken care of me and my family and will keep doing so. Show me how to be generous in my thoughts, words, and deeds.

SPIRITUAL FATHERS AND MOTHERS

Read 2 Timothy 1

KEY VERSE:

I am reminded of your sincere faith, which first lived in your grandmother Lois and in your mother Eunice and, I am persuaded, now lives in you also.

2 TIMOTHY 1:5 NIV

UNDERSTAND:

Think about any adults (besides your relatives) who greatly impacted your life and faith. What made them special, and which of their qualities did you want to emulate?

....

....

....

What adults do your children have relationships with besides you? What kind of people are those adults?

....

....

....

Why might it be important to have other adults besides you to speak into your kids' lives? How could you foster those relationships?

....

....

....

APPLY:

After Paul shared his story and the good news of Jesus with them, Timothy and his mother (Eunice) and his grandmother (Lois) all became Christians. Scripture makes no mention of Timothy's father or grandfather; they may have died when the boy was young. But ultimately, God provided a spiritual father in Paul. While the apostle mentored him in faith, Timothy encouraged Paul and gave him friendship and companionship.

Our children need other adults in their circles besides us who can speak truth and love, listen to them, and be a safe place. Whether we reside near a large extended clan or we're solo parents who live far from relatives, God will be faithful to provide.

Practically, this first looks like praying for our children to find and form relationships with godly men and women. Second, once we've reached a level of trust, we can be bold in reaching out to those adults and asking for their prayers and presence. They'll most likely be honored that we asked.

....

....

....

....

....

....

....

PRAY:

Father, as You provided Paul for Timothy, I'm asking You to provide godly, trustworthy spiritual mentors for my kids. Help me be intentional about forming relationships with other adults who can show my children what it looks like to follow Jesus day-to-day. May my kids emulate You but also those people who serve You faithfully and tenaciously.

ALL FOR OUR GOOD

Read Genesis 50

KEY VERSE:

"You intended to harm me, but God intended it all for good. He brought me to this position so I could save the lives of many people."

Genesis 50:20 NLT

UNDERSTAND:

Picture a hard situation from the past that God used for good in your life.

....

....

....

....

....

....

Pray about a difficult circumstance your child or relative is facing, and ask God to bring about His purposes.

....

....

....

....

....

....

....

APPLY:

God's knowledge is far greater than ours. He can take a heart-wrenching situation—like Joseph being unjustly thrown in jail—and turn it into a glory far greater than we could imagine. He used every part of Joseph's life to prepare him to be the leader he needed to be. And He gave up His own Son in the ultimate redemption story, in which the betrayed Savior went from a cross to a crown, and those who believe went from death to life.

All of it gives us a picture of a God who is intricately aware of His children's lives and who makes a way for His plans to prevail—for His glory and our good. What a comfort! The God who molded the galaxies and keeps the planet turning at just the right speed and perfect distance from the sun—this God, who created the world and all that it holds, created and keeps us and our children too.

....

....

....

....

....

....

....

....

....

....

PRAY:

You are the Creator of all, and You will work every situation for Your purposes and my good. Help me to trust Your plans for me and my family, especially when they don't make sense to me. I know that I have limited understanding, and that Your ways and thoughts are higher than mine.

THE PAIN (AND BEAUTY) OF LETTING GO

Read Exodus 2

KEY VERSES:

The woman conceived and bore a son, and when she saw that he was a fine child, she hid him three months. When she could hide him no longer, she took for him a basket made of bulrushes and daubed it with bitumen and pitch. She put the child in it and placed it among the reeds by the river bank.

Exodus 2:2–3 ESV

UNDERSTAND:

In what ways are you fighting or struggling to let go of your child?

....

....

....

....

....

What might God want to teach you in this season?

....

....

....

....

....

....

APPLY:

Jochebed, an Israelite mother who hid her baby son, Moses, from a murderous ruler and then entrusted him to the Nile and the God she served, sent his big sister to watch over him and report back to Jochebed what was happening.

God provided the daughter of that same hard-hearted ruler to snatch the baby from harm's way. He blessed Miriam's quick thinking and placed Moses back in his mother's arms for a time. And He saved Moses so that Moses could, when the time was right, lead His chosen people out of slavery and into freedom.

Jochebed couldn't understand everything God asked her to endure, but she was faithful and eventually saw the fulfillment of God's astonishing plans.

Like her, one day, we will see the rest of the story and proclaim our praises to God. No matter how difficult it is to release a child, let's resolve to pray for discernment, peace, and grace.

....

....

....

....

....

....

....

....

....

PRAY:

God, I have a hard time letting go of my child. Seeing them walk away from me and not being able to protect them from the world frightens me. Give me discernment, peace, and grace to be able to release them into Your perfect and tender care. Thank You for loving them even more than I do.

STAYING IN THE GAME

Read 2 Chronicles 15

KEY VERSE:

"But as for you, be strong and do not lose courage, for there is reward for your work."

2 CHRONICLES 15:7 AMP

UNDERSTAND:

Which part of the daily grind of motherhood is most difficult for you?

Who might pray for and with you about gaining strength for the challenging moments of parenthood?

APPLY:

One mom with three children under age six admits, "For me, on a day when the kids struggle to listen to me, when I'm hearing my own voice guiding and instructing them all day with little obedience. . .I want so badly to just [mentally and emotionally] check out."

How do we consistently instruct, remain calm, and stay "in the game"? Our work can be repetitive (and sometimes boring), we get little thanks, and children aren't always the best conversationalists. Just as the prophet Azariah encouraged Asa as he removed idols and began following the Lord, other godly moms can encourage us to remain faithful.

Daily, let's pray for God to infuse us with His strength and vision. Let's also remind ourselves about the rewards of teaching obedience. When we guide our kids to follow God and respect His ways, it reaps rewards for their lives and those God places in their paths. Not only that, we'll also see benefits in eternity that we can only dream of now.

....

....

....

....

....

....

....

....

....

PRAY:

Father, I am tempted to give in to apathy and discouragement in the daily grind of motherhood. Infuse me with Your perfect strength and vision as I parent. Daily remind me about the benefits of teaching my children to follow and obey You. I can't wait to see the eternal rewards You will show in Your goodness and grace.

IT'S ALL WORTH IT

Read John 12

KEY VERSE:

"Truly, truly, I say to you, unless a grain of wheat falls into the earth and dies, it remains alone; but if it dies, it bears much fruit."

JOHN 12:24 ESV

UNDERSTAND:

What sacrifices of motherhood are especially difficult for you to make? Why?

....

....

....

....

....

....

In what ways is God asking you to die to yourself during the season you're in?

....

....

....

....

....

....

....

APPLY:

The late nights, prayers soaked in tears, money sacrificed, hours in the car and at events, times we impart discipline in love (even when they don't "get it"), and long moments spent listening to them talk about everything and nothing—every minute invested in your child's growth and spiritual formation is a seed planted.

We may not see the outcome of it all, but when they reach young adulthood, we might start to recognize a few fruits. Our kids then become friends who cheer us on. Some of them pray for us when we need it. They—*gasp!*—at times listen to our advice and take it. They pursue their own passions; and somehow, in God's alchemy, their wins become ours and are ten times better than if we'd won.

And even if we don't see any of those outward signs of growth, not a second planted in sacrificial love for our children is wasted. It's always worth it.

PRAY:

Father, show me what it means to die to myself.
May my sacrifices be seeds You water. When I'm exhausted,
remind me that everything I do in service to those I love is
for You—and will be more than worth it in the end.

HE'LL NEVER SAY GOODBYE

Read John 14

KEY VERSE:

"Peace I leave with you; my peace I give to you; I do not give it to you as the world does. Do not let your hearts be distressed or lacking in courage."

JOHN 14:27 NET

UNDERSTAND:

Which goodbyes have been hardest for you as a mom? Which future goodbyes are you dreading?

....

....

....

....

....

....

How might it help you to picture God standing with you in those moments?

....

....

....

....

....

....

APPLY:

Whether we're kissing a child's forehead before leaving her in a NICU, dropping him off at preschool, giving her a high five before she enters middle school, or driving away after setting up his college dorm room, we moms have to say goodbye to our children far more often than we might expect.

However, our hurting hearts can take comfort from today's key verse. Though Jesus was about to leave His disciples and return to His Father in heaven, He was not leaving them to do life on their own. Instead, He would leave the Holy Spirit—the third person of the Trinity—with His followers to comfort and guide them. The Holy Spirit imparts peace, insight, and wisdom as we attune our hearts to His presence.

Want someone in your life who will never say goodbye? Friend, that's Jesus. He not only gives us the Holy Spirit to comfort and teach us, He also indwells us with His very life.

....

....

....

....

....

....

....

....

....

PRAY:

Precious Jesus, thank You that Your indwelling presence will never leave or forsake me. I'm so grateful also for the Holy Spirit, who gives me peace and instructs me and my children. It means everything that You will never say farewell to us and that we never have to say goodbye to You.

A SINGLE-MINDED FOCUS

Read Jeremiah 32

KEY VERSE:

"Then I will give them one heart and one way, that they may fear Me forever, for the good of them and their children after them."
JEREMIAH 32:39 NKJV

UNDERSTAND:

How might your single-minded focus on the things of God be good for your children?

....

....

....

....

....

....

In what ways could you become more single-minded in pursuing Him? (As a start, think about your thoughts, words, and daily actions.)

....

....

....

....

....

....

....

APPLY:

In today's passage, God revealed to the prophet Jeremiah that the Israelites would be conquered and exiled because of their habitual sin. In the same proclamation, though, He promised to one day bring them back and give them prosperity. What a faithful God we serve—one who sees our sin and at the same time loves us so fiercely that He cannot help but provide a way for us to reconcile with Him.

God is not only faithful and providential but has the power to give us singleness of heart and mind so that we are more like Him. With His help, we can model a healthy fear of the Lord to our children while still giving them grace when they sin.

In a culture that seeks to distract us at every turn—*Make more money! Seek success over integrity! Get offended by everything!*—let's pursue Him diligently so we can be laser-focused on Jesus.

PRAY:

Forgive me, Lord, for being distracted so often from the purposes and plans You have for me. As a mom, I want to be singly focused on Jesus and Your Word so I can teach my children by word, deed, and example how beautiful and awesome You are. Thank You for beginning and sustaining this work in me by Your grace.

MOTHERHOOD: A REFINING FIRE

Read Psalm 66

KEY VERSE:

For You, God, tested us; You refined us as silver is refined.

PSALM 66:10 HCSB

UNDERSTAND:

Think about difficult circumstances several biblical characters went through. How did they grow (or not grow) in their faith as a result?

How has a difficult season from your past strengthened your faith?

APPLY:

Along with marriage, parenthood can be a way God refines our heart and shows us the depth of our selfishness. All it takes is becoming a mother to realize what we *thought* was our godliness was instead the fact that we were rarely interrupted, challenged, or disobeyed.

Just as silver and gold are purified at an extremely high heat, being a mother often puts us in difficult circumstances in which we realize our need for God. However, if we'll surrender to the refining process, we will find that God takes our stubbornness and transforms it into a realization that He is far more patient and forgiving with us than we are with others.

And we need not be afraid that the heating of our souls will destroy us, for as the *Cultural Backgrounds Study Bible* notes about Proverbs 17:3, "The refining process requires expertise and *an intimate knowledge of the tools and metals involved.*" Thank the Lord! He knows exactly how—and how long—to test us.

....

....

....

....

....

....

....

....

....

PRAY:

Heavenly Father, forgive me for my stubbornness and selfishness. I surrender to Your refining work in my life. When my children test my patience and cause me frustration, turn my heart and mind to prayer. Remind me that the hard things about motherhood are purifying my desires and making me more like Jesus.

TRUST GOD WITH YOUR TEARS

Read Psalm 56

KEY VERSE:

You have taken account of my wanderings; put my tears in Your bottle. Are they not recorded in Your book?
Psalm 56:8 AMP

UNDERSTAND:

Why do you think the psalmists could be so honest with God?

Are you honest with God in your own relationship with Him? Why or why not?

APPLY:

Dealing with anxiety, depression, OCD, ADHD, and other illnesses can put a strain on the strongest families. As moms, our hearts break when we see our children struggle in school, relationships, and with their own thoughts and emotions. It feels unfair and cruel.

That's why the Psalms are precious to scores of believers. They show an honest relationship with God and give us hope for the future. While there are celebratory psalms, many of the psalmists wrote of their sorrow, grief, doubt, questions, and despair. Their honesty shows that God is not afraid of our pain.

In the meantime, know that God also provides trained physicians, medicine, counseling, the Holy Spirit, trusted friends, and loved ones to come alongside us as we work to find answers.

Be encouraged, friend: Our Father cares about your struggle—and your child's struggle. He is with and for you, and He can be trusted with your anguish.

PRAY:

Thank You for caring about our grief and keeping track of our tears. My heart is heavy as I watch my child struggle. Father, I know You love him. Please show us how best to help him. Send us the right people and tools so he can begin healing and finally thrive instead of just survive.

WHO ARE YOU LISTENING TO?

Read Proverbs 12

KEY VERSE:

The way of a fool is right in his own opinion,
but the one who listens to advice is wise.
PROVERBS 12:15 NET

UNDERSTAND:

Where do you go for advice and input: online, friends, relatives, fellow believers?

How much input do you receive from godly people you know well?

How much input do you receive daily from God's Word? (Be honest!)

APPLY:

Some of us fill our ears with input from social media influencers whose motives may be mixed. Others read books published by self-help authors who may or may not take God's Word into consideration. That's why it's important to be choosy about whose advice we listen to. Wise people listen to the right advice.

That's because not all advice is *good* advice. Trusted input should mostly come from women you know and whose godly character and integrity you've seen in person over several years.

Ask an older mom in your church whose adult children are world changers to lunch or coffee. Tell her how much you admire her family and ask her about her parenting journey. Or invite a fellow mom who lives with joy after a season of hardship to your house for an afternoon and get to know her. In this way, you can cultivate both a friendship and wisdom.

....

....

....

....

....

....

....

....

....

....

PRAY:

Lord, I want to be a wise woman. Give me discernment to filter out any unbiblical advice, and show me women in my church and community who exhibit godly characteristics. Help me to have courage to ask them to give me input so I can surround myself with wisdom.

THE PRAISE OF CHILDREN

Read Psalm 8

KEY VERSE:

Because of Your adversaries, You have established a stronghold from the mouths of children and nursing infants to silence the enemy and the avenger.

PSALM 8:2 HCSB

UNDERSTAND:

Think of a time your child delighted you with an observation about God or nature (or both). What did they say?

Why do you think Jesus loved children and encouraged them to enjoy and delight in Him?

APPLY:

It's interesting that the Hebrew word for "stronghold/strength" in today's key verse can also be translated as "praise." You wouldn't think of kids as having strength in battle, would you? They're physically the weakest of humans. However, the psalmist wrote that God created worship from babies and children to silence His enemies.

Jesus was drawn to children and often drew them to Himself, even rebuking those who tried to dissuade the little ones from enjoying His presence. Perhaps we should take a note from our Savior.

As moms, we get impatient with our kids' endless questions and observations, many of which we don't know the answers to. However, children are open to spiritual things with their innocence, wonder, and lack of cynicism. Maybe instead of rushing through the next conversation, we can go deeper with them and ask them what they think. We might be surprised and delighted into praising God ourselves; we might even gain strength for our next battle.

....

....

....

....

....

....

....

....

....

PRAY:

Lord, give me patience next time my children want to talk endlessly. Help me see their lack of cynicism and their innocence as doorways to worship and awe. Show me how to mirror their excitement about ordinary things, that I might see Your creation more fully and revere You more extravagantly.

THE ONE WHO NEVER FAILS

Read Deuteronomy 31

KEY VERSE:

"Do not be afraid or discouraged, for the Lord will personally go ahead of you. He will be with you; he will neither fail you nor abandon you."

Deuteronomy 31:8 NLT

UNDERSTAND:

When your child is going through suffering, what do you feel? What do you think? How do you pray?

....

....

....

....

....

....

Who and what could you bring around you to strengthen you so you can be strong for your child?

....

....

....

....

....

....

APPLY:

Moses wasn't allowed to go with the people of Israel into the Promised Land, so in the latter part of Deuteronomy, he gave them encouragement for the journey. In a similar way, we moms are not allowed to "go with" our children into every situation. They might experience relationship breakups, school stress, chronic pain, or many other difficulties. And whether it is physical or mental anguish, it's often harder to see our kids suffer than to suffer ourselves.

In those times of struggle, it's imperative that we lean on God and other people. The Word, worship music, gatherings with loved ones who know our heartache, and time in nature can comfort and strengthen us so we can be strong for our children.

Remember also that God goes with and before and behind us—and our children. He is always present and ever faithful. May that give you courage to face whatever tomorrow brings.

....

....

....

....

....

....

....

....

....

PRAY:

I want to be with my child always, Father, but that's not the way it works. Thank You for being with her wherever she goes. Encourage my heart and remind me of Your faithfulness and love for her. Give me strength so I can, in turn, impart strength and courage to her.

HOW TO LIVE WITH HOPE

Read Isaiah 26

KEY VERSE:

"You will keep in perfect and constant peace the one whose mind is steadfast [that is, committed and focused on You—in both inclination and character], Because he trusts and takes refuge in You [with hope and confident expectation]."

Isaiah 26:3 AMP

UNDERSTAND:

What worries keep you up at night? Write them down, confessing them to God.

What scriptural promises (like Isaiah 26:3) could you memorize to repeat back to yourself when you start to derail into fear?

APPLY:

Mothers fret about the little things (*When will our baby's teething pain stop?*) and the big (*Will our teenager's rebellion end in disaster?*). That's why it's imperative that we go to the Word in every season and circumstance. Isaiah 26:3 is a reminder that our minds will rest *if* our focus is on God.

Scholar Matthew Henry put it this way: "For in the *Lord Jehovah-Jah, Jehovah*, in him who was, and is, and is to come, there is a rock of ages, a firm and lasting foundation for faith and hope to build upon; and the house built on that rock will stand in a storm. Those that trust in God shall not only find in him, but receive *from him, everlasting strength*, strength that will carry them to everlasting life, to that blessedness which is forever; and therefore let them trust in him forever, and never cast away nor change their confidence."

....

....

....

....

....

....

....

....

....

....

PRAY:

Father, I want to be committed and focused on You in both my inclination and character. Help me trust in You with hope and confident expectation. Thank You for your supernatural peace that is constant amid ever-changing circumstances. You are my refuge and strength, a firm and lasting foundation.

DELIGHT IN HIS WORD

Read Psalm 1

KEY VERSE:

But his delight is in the law of the Lord,
and on his law he meditates day and night.
Psalm 1:2 ESV

UNDERSTAND:

Would you say that you honestly delight in God's Word? Why or why not?

What would help you find more joy in spending time with the Bible?

Who do you know that takes daily sustenance from scripture? How might they encourage you?

APPLY:

The Bible is a book of many different genres, full of historical documents recorded by servants of God with cultural backgrounds much different than ours. It can overwhelm and intimidate us. However, as believers we have a "secret weapon" in our quest to understand and apply God's Word: the Holy Spirit.

Determine to begin a lifelong study right where you are. You could start with these five practical questions:

- Who is speaking in the passage?
- Who is the audience for the passage?
- What is the cultural and historical context of the passage?
- What does this passage teach me about God?
- How can I apply this passage to my life?

Our Father promises to impart wisdom, joy, and peace when we're diligent to open the book He penned through faithful people. And here's a bonus: When you make it a place to run to instead of run from, your children will also reap the benefits.

PRAY:

I long to love Your beautiful Word, Father. Teach me to delight in it instead of being overwhelmed and intimidated. Holy Spirit, guide me as I read and digest scriptures, showing me where to stop, ponder, and ask questions. May I never tire of feasting on its riches.

THE POWER OF A MOM'S WORDS

Read Ephesians 4

KEY VERSE:

Do not let any unwholesome talk come out of your mouths, but only what is helpful for building others up according to their needs, that it may benefit those who listen.

EPHESIANS 4:29 NIV

UNDERSTAND:

What's one of the best things someone ever said to you? Who said it?

What's one of the worst things someone ever said to you? Who said it?

Which words come more naturally to you—sarcastic, cutting words or life-giving, sweet words?

APPLY:

Some of the most powerful and life-lasting words are those spoken by parents over their children. We can bless or curse, empower or diminish, and cheer or enrage our children just by speaking to them.

Each of us remember the best and worst things people have said to us, especially if they came from a parent.

Moms can set the tone of a child's day or night with upbeat, positive words. We can comfort our son's hurting heart with compassionate, empathetic words. And we can give our daughter wings to soar with—words like "I'm proud of you," "I'm in your corner," or "I love you exactly the way you are."

No matter your personality, you can ask God to help you control what comes out of your mouth, especially in times of frustration. Because His divine intent is to make us like Christ, He will transform us in thoughts, words, and deeds when we daily surrender to Him.

....

....

....

....

....

....

....

....

....

PRAY:

Lord, forgive me when I use cutting words in response to my children. I want to build them up and not tear them down. Give me more compassion, empathy, and patience, and help me be careful when I speak. May my child feel seen, known, and completely loved—just as I am in You.

WISDOM FOR DECISIONS

Read Proverbs 3

KEY VERSE:

Wisdom is more precious than rubies;
nothing you desire can compare with her.
PROVERBS 3:15 NLT

UNDERSTAND:

Does making decisions come naturally to you, or do you find it difficult?

What decision(s) are you or your family members facing right now?

How do you usually make decisions?

APPLY:

Pastor and author Andy Stanley says he asks himself five questions when he needs to decide something important. He teaches his children to ask them too whenever they come to a fork in the road and the answer isn't immediately obvious:

- Why am I doing this, really?
- What story do I want to tell someday about this season or about me?
- Is there a tension here that deserves my attention?
- What is the wise thing to do considering my past experiences, current circumstances, and future hopes and dreams?
- What does love (of God and others) require of me?[1]

We would do well to teach those questions to our kids and to use them ourselves. After all, if we can step outside ourselves and discern our motives, emotions, and scriptural truth, it will make the choice between two alternatives much clearer. We might even save ourselves from heartache and regret.

....

....

....

....

PRAY:

So many decisions come up for my family members, Lord, and I don't always have the wisdom to help them. However, I know You promise to give me guidance and discernment. Help me to make time to develop our relationship so I can glean from Your wisdom and hear Your voice speaking to me.

[1] Stanley related these questions in an interview on the May 18, 2022 episode of *The Alli Worthington Show* podcast.

WHEN HEALING DOESN'T COME

Read James 5

KEY VERSE:

Is anyone among you suffering? Let him pray.
Is anyone cheerful? Let him sing psalms.
JAMES 5:13 NKJV

UNDERSTAND:

What prayers for healing have not been answered in the way you would like?

....

....

....

....

....

....

How has that affected your relationship with God?

....

....

....

....

....

....

....

APPLY:

During Jesus' short earthly ministry, He showed extravagant love in each place He journeyed by healing people. By the power of His hand, the blind saw, the deaf heard, the lame walked and even leapt—and the sick found they were suddenly, miraculously well.

Many moms find motherhood even more challenging than normal because we live with an illness. For some, it's invisible and people don't understand how we could be sick. We pray for physical healing, but it doesn't come. We wonder what God is up to and why He chooses not to answer that prayer with "yes."

Long-term suffering like living with illness and pain can make us question God's goodness. Thankfully, we have many examples in scripture of people sharing those kinds of doubts and frustrations with the one who knows us best. Today, try not to turn away from Jesus in your questioning. Instead, press into the relationship. He will meet you and sustain you for the long haul of parenthood.

PRAY:

Draw me close to You when I don't understand what You're doing, Father. Help me not to run away in frustration or doubt but instead pray honestly about my hopes, fears, and questions. You promise that You will draw near to me when I draw near to You, and I need You now.

JEHOVAH-RAPHA, OUR HEALER

Read Exodus 15

KEY VERSE:

"If you listen carefully to the LORD your God and do what is right in his eyes, if you pay attention to his commands and keep all his decrees, I will not bring on you any of the diseases I brought on the Egyptians, for I am the LORD, who heals you."

EXODUS 15:26 NIV

UNDERSTAND:

Have you grumbled or complained lately about something? What is it?

Do you truly trust God fully in that situation? What might your actions say about your answer?

APPLY:

Today's passage reveals one of God's names in scripture: *Jehovah-Rapha*, "the Lord Who Heals." During the forty years the Israelites spent in the wilderness, they ended up in the Desert of Shur, where they spent three days without finding water. They did eventually find water, but it was so bitter they couldn't quench their thirst with it. Then the exhausted and dehydrated children of Israel grumbled and complained, revealing a greater problem than thirst: bitterness of soul.

Still, as their leader, Moses prayed. God had mercy on His people and told Moses to throw a nearby piece of wood in the water. Suddenly, the water became clean or "healed" so the people could drink.

Friend, what part of you is thirsty today? Where do you (or one of your kids) need healing? Lift that place to Jehovah-Rapha in prayer, trusting that He is still the God who turns bitter things sweet and provides miraculously for His children's needs.

PRAY:

There are needs all around me, and sometimes they feel too big for even You, Lord. Forgive me for not trusting You for what my family and I need. You are Jehovah-Rapha, and You promise us provision, peace, healing, and mercy when we lean on You. May it be so.

SABBATH, THE VERY GOOD IDEA

Read Genesis 2

KEY VERSE:

And on the seventh day God finished his work that he had done, and he rested on the seventh day from all his work that he had done.

GENESIS 2:2 ESV

UNDERSTAND:

Do you currently keep a Sabbath (a time during the week devoted to worship, rest, and other life-giving activities)? Why or why not?

Jesus fulfilled the law, so why should Christians keep the Sabbath? What do we gain from regularly resting from work and busyness?

APPLY:

It's not easy to keep a Sabbath. Years ago, states had "blue laws" on the books so that stores were closed on Sunday. Now, Sundays are business as usual. Our kids may have activities on Sundays, or we (or our husbands) need to work.

Still, God created the Sabbath because He made us to need rest. It's like a spiritual and physical reset button. And once you've put into place a weekly or regular Sabbath and experienced its affects, you'll be amazed at the difference you feel.

Talk with your family about fun, restful things you could implement on Sunday or another day of the week: naps, playing games, taking a walk, making a craft, getting together with friends. Think about what brings you joy and helps you take a deep breath after a long workweek. As you experience a Sabbath, you'll see why it is one of God's very good ideas.

PRAY:

Creator God, You rested on the seventh day and made me to need rest also. I know I don't give myself enough permission to cease from housework, paying bills, job requirements, and various activities. I'm tired, and I can feel myself needing a regular weekly pause. Give me the creativity and discipline to institute a Sabbath for myself and my family.

MOMS NEED TO PLAY

Read Proverbs 31

KEY VERSE:

She is clothed with strength and dignity,
and she laughs without fear of the future.
PROVERBS 31:25 NLT

UNDERSTAND:

Name a few qualities of the woman Solomon described in today's passage. Which would you most like to emulate? Which do you think you already possess?

Why could she laugh without fear of the future? What does that say about her faith?

The passage most likely describes a woman's entire life, so keep that in mind as you study it. Don't let the volume or variety of her actions intimidate you.

APPLY:

For sure, the Proverbs 31 woman worked hard, but she may have played hard as well. Playing involves laughter, imagination, movement, and relationships—all wonderful, life-giving gifts from our Creator. Perhaps Jesus was drawn to children because of the fierceness of their creativity and love of play.

Too many of us think growing up means growing out of the need to play. But play helps us learn and grow. The most well-balanced adults paint, join a softball team, do community theater, or practice an instrument. However, most of us spend far too many hours behind a computer screen or on the couch logged into a device (guilty!).

This week, make a list of those things you were passionate about as a young person. Chances are, one of those is a perfect place to start fitting regular play into your life. And if you have young children, why not join them the next time they say, "Play with me, Momma!"? You might just have fun.

PRAY:

Creator, thank You for Your gifts of laughter, movement, relationships, imagination, and creativity. Help me to remember what I loved as a child, knowing that "playing" might help me reconnect with fun and adventure. Show me the value of getting on my knees or on the floor with my kids, joining them in play.

TAKE COURAGE FROM BIBLICAL MOTHERS

Read Luke 1

KEY VERSE:

And Mary said, "Behold, I am the servant of the Lord; let it be to me according to your word." And the angel departed from her.

LUKE 1:38 ESV

UNDERSTAND:

Which biblical moms inspire you? Why?

....

....

....

....

....

....

....

Which biblical mothers would you like to learn more about?

....

....

....

....

....

....

....

APPLY:

The Bible is full of courageous mothers like Sarah, who became the mother of Isaac and the people of Israel, and Mary, whose obedience to God led to her bearing and raising the Messiah. Other scriptural mothers provide inspiration and encouragement as we see how God took their ordinary lives and used them for His glory—and to further His story.

Role models like those biblical mothers inspire us to make wise choices and to keep moving forward despite life's inevitable failures and disappointments. While we shouldn't worship the women we consider heroes, we can learn from their journeys.

Why not pick one or two biblical mothers and dig deep into studying their lives? Ask God to reveal character traits you can emulate and other things you might need to work on. After all, whether you realize it or not, *you're* a role model to your children. In that way, God is already mightily using you.

....

....

....

....

....

....

....

....

....

PRAY:

Father, thank You for the example of women like Hannah, Sarah, Mary, Lois, Eunice, and so many other biblical women. I'm grateful for their lives of courage and faith. Help me to be a godly example of motherhood to my own children.

THE POWER OF A MOM'S PRAYER

Read James 5

KEY VERSE:

Therefore confess your sins to each other and pray for each other so that you may be healed. The prayer of a righteous person is powerful and effective.

JAMES 5:16 NIV

UNDERSTAND:

Who do you consider to be a warrior in prayer? Do you consider yourself more a warrior or worrier? Why is that?

....

....

....

....

....

....

Do you feel like your prayers are powerful and effective? (Spoiler alert: They are!)

....

....

....

....

....

....

APPLY:

When we look at chaotic events like natural disasters, wars, political scandals, and financial meltdowns, it's easy to feel helpless and hopeless. However, as moms we are not powerless because no matter the circumstances that surround us and our families, we can always pray. Prayer is an affirmation that God is on His throne and the things happening around us don't surprise or dismay Him.

In God's upside-down kingdom, the most powerful place to be is on our knees—interceding and pleading.

Pray for peace in our nations, cities, and world. Pray for the hungry to be fed and the sick to be healed. Pray for our churches, pastors, and Christian leaders. And pray like crazy for our children—for their health, decision-making, and friends. Pray about their school, activities, future spouse, and career path. Pray especially for their faith to grow daily and their relationship with God to be the most important thing in their lives.

....

....

....

....

....

....

....

....

....

PRAY:

Heavenly Father, I want to be a prayer warrior. Teach me the power of prayer for my children, husband, church, city, and world. Show me specific things to pray for, and guide me through Your Holy Spirit who intercedes for me. Thank You that my prayers will do more than worries ever could.

BE STRONG

Read Isaiah 35

KEY VERSES:

Strengthen the feeble hands, steady the knees that give way; say to those with fearful hearts, "Be strong, do not fear; your God will come. . .to save you."

Isaiah 35:3–4 NIV

UNDERSTAND:

Do you have fears that keep you up at night? What are they?

Do you struggle with anxiety that paralyzes you? Would you be willing to ask for help for it?

APPLY:

Just like children are afraid of the dark, we moms have fears that strangle our joy and cause our hearts to race. What if something happens to our kid? What if our husband is unfaithful? What if we lose our job? What if there's a natural disaster near us? The questions can overwhelm and even paralyze us once we give them permission to inhabit our minds.

That's why it's imperative that we allow God to lead us to healing. First, we need to turn off the news and tune into scripture and music that encourages us to trust Him. Second, if our fears keep us from engaging fully in life, we may need professional help to rule out underlying physical and mental issues that can cause anxiety and panic.

Let's not be too proud to ask for help from God and others. He is faithful to strengthen and empower the weak in a variety of ways.

....

....

....

....

....

....

....

....

....

....

PRAY:

Sometimes my fears threaten to overwhelm me, God. Help me to humble myself and ask for help—from my husband and loved ones, and from other trained individuals—if I need it. Most of all, thank You that You promise to strengthen the weak and give courage to the feeble-hearted.

FEEL FREE TO LAMENT

Read Psalm 6

KEY VERSE:

Have mercy on me, Lord, for I am faint;
heal me, Lord, for my bones are in agony.
Psalm 6:2 NIV

UNDERSTAND:

Do you feel free to tell God when you're angry at him? Why or why not?

Did you know over one-third of the Psalms are categorized as lament? (Psalm 6 is one of those.) What do you think that says about God?

APPLY:

There are times when our circumstances press down on us with such force that all we can do is cry out to God in anguish. Whether it's a sudden loss, scary diagnosis, or any number of other issues, our souls can become so heavy that, like the psalmist, we feel faint.

Thankfully, God's Word includes honest passages that portray people of great faith (among them Elijah, Job, and Jesus) in the throes of agonizing sorrow. The Psalms in particular span the gamut from thunderous praise to howling grief. The many psalms of lament give us language with which to seek after God, even during horrifying situations.

Let the fact that intense grief and lament are included in the Bible encourage you to trust God with your pain. Share with Him your questions, anger, and confusion. He's not waiting to strike you down if you tell Him how you really feel; after all, He already knows.

....

....

....

....

....

....

....

....

....

....

PRAY:

I praise You that You are not a God who turns me away when I ask questions or rail at You in anger or pain. Give me the courage to be authentic and to run toward You and not away from You in those seasons. Thank You for examples of honest prayer in scripture.

GOD WAITS ON US

Read Isaiah 30

KEY VERSE:

Yet the Lord longs to be gracious to you; therefore he will rise up to show you compassion. For the Lord is a God of justice. Blessed are all who wait for him!

Isaiah 30:18 NIV

UNDERSTAND:

Have you ever thought about God waiting? Look up the story of the prodigal son, in which the father represents God. What does this story tell you about Him?

....

....

....

....

....

....

In what way(s) are you waiting on God?

....

....

....

....

....

....

....

APPLY:

God waits for us to acknowledge Him, waits for us to repent of our sins, and waits for us to daily surrender our wills and plans to Him. He doesn't force us to obey but woos us tenderly.

However, in today's key verse, the prophet said that the Lord waits to be gracious and show mercy to us. Does that mean He holds off blessing us until we're good enough? Not at all! In context, the idea seems to be that judgment against the Israelites would bring sorrow to God, so He was willing to wait on judging them and show compassion if they were willing to repent. It also notes that everyone who waits on God will be blessed.

What a beautiful word picture the prophet Isaiah painted here: God waits on us to come to Him, and when we wait on Him to work in our lives, we are blessed. It's a divine circle of provision and blessing.

....

....

....

....

....

....

....

....

....

....

PRAY:

Lord, You are so patient with me. I praise You for Your compassion and grace. Thank You for Your promise of blessing when I trust and obey You. Forgive me for my own impatience. Help me to rely on Your patience, not my own, as I wait on both small and large answers to prayer.

KNOW GOD IS NEAR

Read Psalm 145

KEY VERSE:

The Lord is near to all who call on him,
to all who call on him in truth.
Psalm 145:18 NIV

UNDERSTAND:

Describe in a couple of words how you feel when you are emotionally needy and you don't sense God's presence.

Think about how you indicate your nearby presence (and give comfort) to your children. How might God use similar means to communicate with you?

APPLY:

Sometimes we don't sense God's presence as much as we'd like to. Author Robyn Rison Chapman notes, "I stumbled across a video of my almost two-year-old. He asks for Mommy and looks for me. I say 'hmm' to which he follows with 'okay' and proceeds to play. He just wanted to know I was near. It struck me as I watched it—that's what most of us want, to know our heavenly Father is near."

Today's scripture tells us that God is near to all of us who call on Him in truth. Even though we may not always "feel" God's nearness, we can rest in the certainty that He is always beside us. And just like Robyn's son, when we want that assurance, we can call out to Him. He's a generous and gracious heavenly Father who answers our desires for confirmation and peace in ways that are deeply personal and tender.

....

....

....

....

....

....

....

....

....

....

....

PRAY:

Father, at times I feel the necessity to ask for confirmation of Your presence. Thank You that from the moment I became Your daughter, You have never been far away. When I call to You in honest searching, You answer. I praise You for how personal and tender You are in answering my prayers.

THE DIVINE DIGNITY OF MOTHERHOOD

Read John 13

KEY VERSE:

"Now that I, your Lord and Teacher, have washed your feet, you also should wash one another's feet."

JOHN 13:14 NIV

UNDERSTAND:

Are acts of service difficult for you? Have they been difficult in the past? How has motherhood changed that (for better or worse)?

....

....

....

....

....

....

How might thinking of those acts as filled with "divine dignity" change your perception?

....

....

....

....

....

....

APPLY:

During the last supper Jesus shared with His twelve closest followers, He grabbed a towel, knelt, and took on the task of a slave by washing His disciples' dirty feet. The washing of feet was a common task for servants because of the sandals their masters wore on dusty roads where feet became filthy.

One commentary on the washing of feet, from Biblestudytools.com, relates, "Jesus, conscious of His divine dignity. . .performed for them this lowliest service. His act of humility actually cleansed their hearts of selfish ambition, killed their pride, and taught them the lesson of love."

As moms, we wash our children's feet from the moment of birth until they can wash on their own. We also perform many other servant-hearted roles in our family. Maybe you've never thought of those thankless jobs as being full of "divine dignity" or as spiritually cleansing tasks, but they are. In everything we do, we're teaching our children the lesson of sacrificial love, just like Jesus continues to teach us.

....

....

....

....

....

....

....

....

....

PRAY:

Motherhood has defined my life, Lord. Sometimes I've fought that definition, but I see now that You've been teaching me all along about sacrificing my pride and ambition in the service of love. Fill me with joy at the divine dignity of this role You've given me so I can better represent You to my family.

ABOUT THE AUTHOR

Dena Dyer loves Jesus, her family, all things literary, coffee, and British television. She's been married to her hubby, Carey, for twenty-five wonderful years (and a couple they don't talk about). They have two young adult sons, Jordan and Jackson, and a rescue dog, Sully.

Dena is a speaker and Bible teacher whose articles and tips have appeared in dozens of magazines, such as *Family Circle, Home Life, Focus on the Family,* and *Reader's Digest*. She has written eleven books, including *Grace for the Race: Meditations for Busy Moms, Let the Crow's Feet and Laugh Lines Come,* and *25 Christmas Blessings;* and coauthored four others, including *Love at First Fight: 52 Story-Based Meditations for Married Couples* with her husband and *Wounded Women of the Bible: Finding Hope When Life Hurts* with Tina Samples.

Her passion is sharing words of humor and hope with wounded and weary people, and she enjoys singing on the praise team at the church where her husband is the worship pastor. She spends too much time online and in the fast-food drive-thru, but she and the Lord are working on it. Connect with her on her website, Instagram, or Facebook.